EXEMPLARY BUILDINGS
SUCCESS STORIES
[FROM BRUSSELS]

Racine

Passive social housing on Avenue Dubrucq [018]: this project of 8 social dwellings and a nursery has contributed to revitalizing a neglected area next to a railway as part of the Scheldt-Meuse neighbourhood contract (B architecten).

[TABLE OF CONTENTS]

Passive offices on Avenue Marly [065] (A2M architectes).

Biplan [055]: passive building with residential apartment units around the Bruxelles-Capitale region (Bxleco1, FHW).

EDITO

EXEMPLARY BUILDINGS, A CHALLENGE SUCCESSFULLY MET BY THE CONSTRUCTION INDUSTRY!

156 Exemplary Buildings awarded the Batex label, 371 000 m² of ecologically built or ecologically renovated, energy-efficient buildings, 24 million euros in subsidies supporting half a billion euros of investment. The outcome of the first four "Exemplary Buildings" calls for proposals is impressive! It places the Brussels-Capital Region in the top tier of European cities in terms of sustainable construction.

With the fifth call for proposals just completed, it is time to stop and take stock, and realize the magnitude of the revolution that Brussels is experiencing, and share with you these experiences and testimonies.

Yes, we can talk about a real revolution set in motion by this call for projects that I initiated in 2007. Previously, the Brussels Region's building stock had the reputation of an energy sieve. Today, foreign delegations regularly visit our Region and its buildings, which are true models. I am proud of this construction sector which has met the challenge of producing Exemplary Buildings at an acceptable cost.

Because these ultra high energy performance buildings, with a low environmental impact, are also cost-effective and replicable. A key criterion in the call for projects is demonstrating that this high level of requirements is both technically and financially attainable. This has allowed us to encourage the construction industry to go further. With this experience behind us, we have decided to impose the passive standard on all new buildings in the Brussels Region from 2015 onwards. A real challenge, an ambitious goal... and an already proven reality!

Especially as, over the years, we see candidates proposing increasingly innovative projects, going as far as zero energy. Energy performance no longer strikes fear, it can even push out the limits of imagination and propose new solutions that blend harmoniously with their surroundings to create attractive places to live.

It is with initiatives like this one that we have achieved an 18% reduction in average energy consumption in Brussels since 2004. The "Exemplary Buildings" call for projects, the grants scheme, the Energy Challenge, the Employment-Environment Alliances, the Sustainable Neighbourhood contracts, the development of green spaces and citizen participation, all these initiatives are making Brussels into an increasingly sustainable city. Thanks to our joint efforts.

Evelyne Huytebroeck
Brussels Minister of Environment,
Energy and Urban Renewal

INTRO

CALL FOR PROJECTS:
"EXEMPLARY BUILDINGS
(BATEX)"[1]

In 2007, the Brussels-Capital Region started organising calls for projects open to everyone wishing to take part in supporting the construction and refurbishment of "Exemplary Buildings". The intention of the "Batex" scheme is to demonstrate that Brussels architects are capable of achieving excellence in sustainable construction using existing techniques and within a reasonable budget.

Projects are assessed by a panel on the basis of 4 criteria:
– best possible energy efficiency
– lowest possible environmental impact
– the reproducibility and cost effectiveness of the proposed solutions
– the quality of their architectural consistency and how well they blend in with the existing urban landscape.

Of the 245 applications submitted between 2007 and 2011, 156 projects involving more than 371 000 m² of floor space have been subsidised. Successful applicants are given 4 years to complete their projects, which, once the building work has been completed and checked, are then "declared" to be Batex buildings. More information on the current call for projects on the website of Brussels Environment:
www.bruxellesenvironnement.be

[1] The term "Batex" derives from the French "Bâtiments exemplaires".

THIS IS NOT A BOOK ABOUT ARCHITECTURE...

This is a book telling a story of collective work. Its purpose is not to extol any formal innovations, indeed 45% of selected projects involve the refurbishment of existing buildings. Nor is it about out-of-this-world projects – all projects are here in Brussels, waiting for you to go and see them. The book does not present any "ivory eco-tower" or a "radical solve-it-all solution" – each project has its own particular merit in its own particular context.

But what then is the common denominator of all these projects and their owners? The answer is that they have made possible a form of urban adventure through opening the door to sustainable construction in Brussels. These are stories about buildings where lots of "first times" have been attempted, stories about projects, building sites, about sweat and tears, stories about pioneers. And even if some did not get it right first time, nine out of ten are saying that they would willingly start all over again.

In a nutshell, though the Batex experiment is set to come up with some attractive architecture, it is first and foremost exemplary for the many new avenues opened up. We have collected this collective know-how and sought to make it readable.

EXEMPLARY?

Does exemplary mean something worthy of being reproduced? Just a few years ago, you would not have found any building in Brussels exemplifying eco-construction. But since 2007 and the birth of Batex, the number of "examples" has greatly increased, with their primary merit being that they have actually been built and are now being lived in! They demonstrate that technical and financial resources are ready and waiting for construction and refurbishment projects meeting high energy, environmental and architectural standards. Concepts are now much more detailed, backed up by real and carefully monitored buildings.

Brussels has now become the place to visit for some of the most sustainable building in the whole of Europe. This is no reason to "faire le dikkenek[2]"! But the fact remains that, whether in the form of new or refurbished houses or apartment buildings, commercial buildings or public amenities, ranging from crèches and schools to sports centres or even a mosque, "sustainability" is being built in Brussels. Or to put it differently, there are now 156 new shades of green in sustainable architecture in Brussels. And the upcoming 2012 Batex round is set to add even more...

We would like to extend our thanks here to all project owners, architects, consultant engineers, companies and residents (and Brussels Environmental Agency employees) who participated in these calls for projects and in particular those kind enough to share their experience.

Bernard Deprez and Jean Cech,
editors

[2] Brussels expression meaning being cocky or showing off.

[009] Nys

[115] De Rinck

[097] Brutopia

[032] Van Volxem

[054] Besme

[090] Libre-Examen

[092] Sébastopol

[134] Moreau

[106] Fort

[046] Droguerie

[052] Lisbonne

[034] Midi-Suède
[108] Alchimiste
[050] nESt
[135] Lemmens
[130] Ostende
[022] Atelier Mommaerts
[112] Belle-Vue
[132] Etangs-Noirs
[093] Tazieaux
[045] MaisiE
[042] Savonnerie Heymans
[018] Dubrucq
[044] De Vrière
[072] CHU Saint-Pierre
[095] Pierre Strauwen
[091] Fineau
[061] Florair
[153] Hectolitre
[118] Vandenbranden
[124] Senne 55
[102] Locquenghien

Public housing, Savonnerie Heymans [042]: inside a city "island", this project has developed semi-public spaces that meet the demands that emerged during the participatory workshops of the Notre Dame au Rouge – Van Artevelde neighbourhood contract. Of the 42 homes, four renovated units in an old building were winners in 2007 (MDW architectes).

ESTABLISHING CONFIDENCE ON THE GROUND

[CHAPTER 01]

For a long time, sustainable construction was on the back burner of political thinking, something to do with personal preferences, details, technology freaks. Then there were all those other prejudices: it's something for the rich, it's too expensive, it doesn't work, there are other social priorities, etc. Among professionals, many saw it merely as an insulation or heating problem, i.e. a construction problem, not an architectural one. In a nutshell, up to now everybody ended up doing his own thing, following his own priorities, incapable of sharing, exchanging and understanding... why.

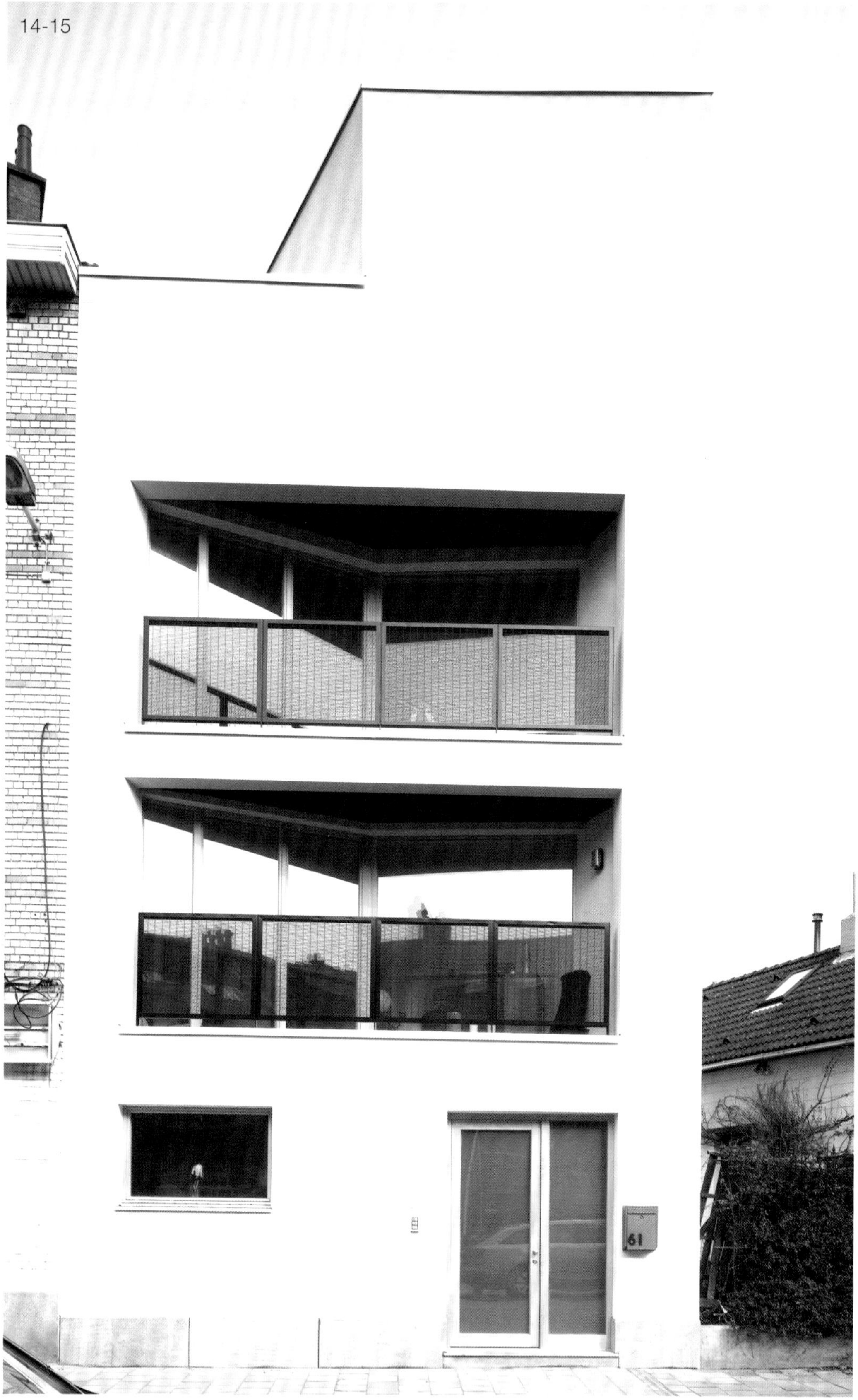

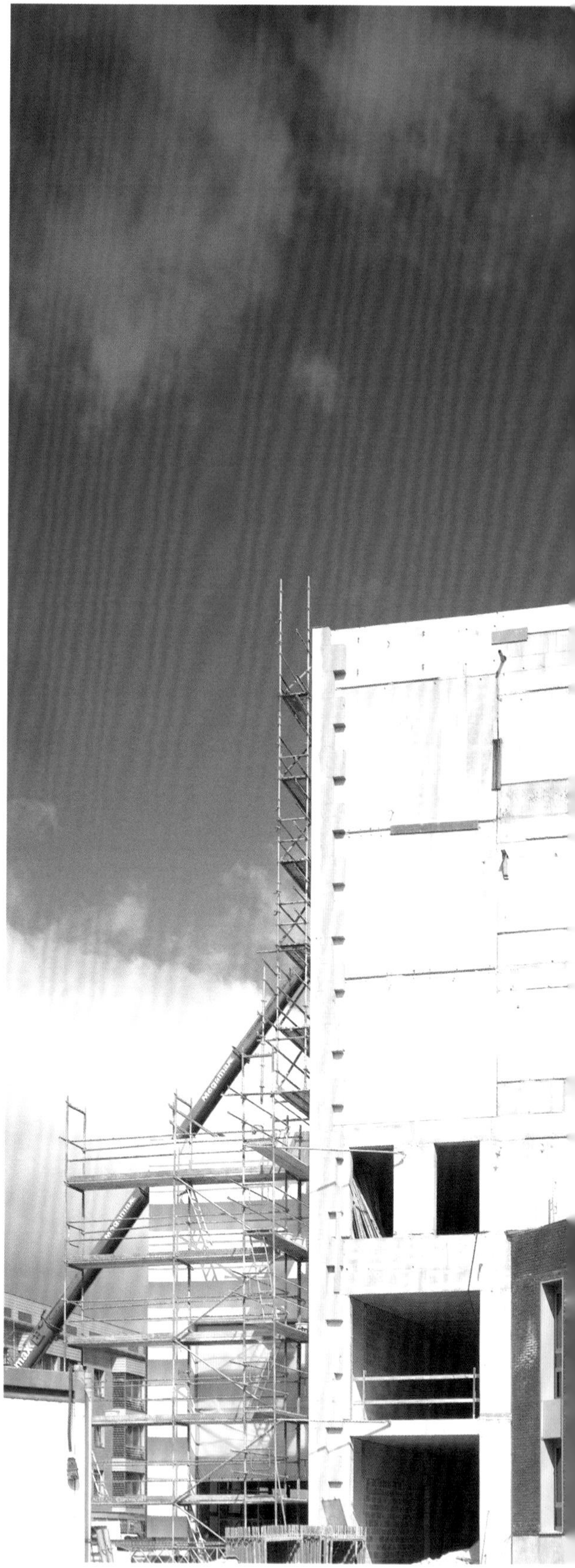

Passive homes, Rue Wauters [017]: these two double-floor apartments will have to wait a long time still for the neighbouring property to be built. The building is almost entirely constructed out of ecological materials. The two façades, intermediate floors and roof are in FSC wood frames with cellulose flakes, rendering on wood fibre insulation and fibre-plaster panels on the inside. The massive front wall is insulated with expanded polystyrene under a final coating (Architect I. Camacho).

Brugmann University Hospital Centre [036]: thanks to their compactness and a high isolation level (from K22 to K31), hospitals appear able to reach top performances in terms of net heating need (Bureau d'architecture E. Verhaegen).

MOVING FORWARDS!

"Owners' demands have changed – for them a passive building is no longer a risky and foolish challenge."
Engineer Denis Lefébure

"In the last twenty years, technology and techniques have developed greatly, meaning that, in contrast to a certain period focusing on mud-and-earth techniques, we can now come up with a very coherent building through selecting the right technologies and techniques and integrating them carefully."
Project owner Benoît Ceysens

"It was an interesting experience. With regard to Law 42 [068] we are still busy digesting the information, as the project was ambitious in more ways than one. We are analysing the results to draw conclusions and identify the interest of each of the project's sustainable aspects."
Architect Sébastien Cruyt

01/ DOING AWAY WITH THE PREJUDICES

Brussels already had a number of "convinced" entrepreneurs, and an eco-construction cluster and a passive building platform were in their initial phases – but what was missing were real-life references where the results did not need to be taken with caution. And then there was no real public discussion forum...

This all changed with the arrival of Batex. Sustainable construction suddenly became something people talked about, a public issue. It slowly became clear how much was at stake, that methods needed to be effective and results convincing. But above all sustainable construction has become a discussion forum in Brussels, where technologies, standards, results, etc. are discussed.

We are learning, we are making progress.

A VISION FOR ACTION

"The current approach, focused on quality and efficiency, is applicable to all our projects in Brussels. And this philosophy doesn't stop at the Region's borders – our projects in the other Regions are benefiting from the maturity now achieved and our accumulated experience with Batex."
Architect Pierre Somers

"The energy-related refurbishment of old buildings in an urban setting with respect for the environment [...] seems to be the path – albeit narrow, not always easy and not catching the media's attention – towards responsible construction."
Architect Marc Opdebeek

Renovation on Rue du Fléron [049]: after 40 years of loyal service, this small house lent itself perfectly to an ambitious eco-renovation (FHW architectes).

Nursery in the Rue Saint-François [071]: facing the Saint-Josse-ten-Node swimming pool, architects 02 delivered in 2011 a nursery with 30 beds and three housing units, following a competition organized as part of the Meridian neighbourhood contract (02 architects).

02/ PUTTING OUT THE CALL

In organising the first call for projects in 2007, the Region's political objective was clear: to disseminate new knowledge, to get professionals and the public at large interested, to demonstrate that it is possible to build differently, more sustainably, more efficiently, and to encourage the sector to get started.

But Batex is not a competition, not a project – it is an appeal. A way of saying that the Region has no detailed answers ready and waiting, but that instead everything will come from the field. The whole idea is that Brussels citizens start thinking about the issue, taking it up and making it their project.

Anyone wanting to work on saving resources – energy, building materials, financial and technical resources – can submit a project, thereby questioning the way we build our homes, our architecture and our city.

Malibran community centre and housing on Rue des Cygnes and Rue de la Digue [039]: Facing north on the Rue de la Digue (keeping the inside of the island for housing) the Community Centre was designed by the architects in collaboration with the residents and can be viewed by passers-by through the wide windows. A glazed brick facing subtly revisits nine-teenth-century industrial architecture (Lpp architects, AAO and Label architecture).

Passive social housing in the Rue de la Brasserie [063]: in the context of the Malibran neighbourhood contract, architects R²D² have "repaired a hollow tooth" with a pro-gramme of 12 passive social dwellings (R²D² architectes).

THE SEARCH
FOR SOCIAL BENEFIT

"To submit a project, it needs to have a social or cultural benefit. It shouldn't just be yet another clever transformation or property development – even if it's green…"
Architect Marc Opdebeek

03/ SUCCESSFUL APPLICANTS WITH THEIR HEARTS IN IT!

All the successful applicants already had a sustainable project in their heads, wanting to reduce their ecological and energy footprint without breaking the bank.

All wanted to enhance the quality of their projects and they were ready to invest a lot of time. They were all financially involved, with the Batex grant nothing more than the icing on the cake – the 24 million euros distributed in the 4 calls represents a mere 5% of the total amount invested by owners themselves.

The call for projects would have remained a dead dog, had not hundreds of private and public / institutional investors themselves had the intention of doing more than the "statutory minimum", sharing the conviction that a habitat with a high environmental quality is a right for everyone. For people working in the field, such as Geert De Pauw from Quartier Bonnevie[1] in Molenbeek, or José Garcia from the tenants' association[2], sustainable construction is not something reserved for the rich. On the contrary, it is a crucial demand that social housing tenants and people on low and not always stable incomes be able to continue living in the city.

[1] www.bonnevie40.be and the Espoir project [060].
[2] The tenants' association awarded the "Golden Brick" to the Loossens [016] project in 2008.

Cédric Polet, architect

A DEVELOPMENT LESSON IN TUNE WITH THE NEIGHBOURHOOD
RUE DU FORT [106]

At the centre of the Alsemberg-Parc neighbourhood contract, the aim of this Régie Foncière (*Housing Fund*) building is to get the neighbouring population to start thinking about sustainable development – something that for many people is still a hollow dream. A somewhat nebulous road to take, given that it is hardly the top priority of those living there...

"In this part of town, people are more receptive to ecological materials and energy savings than they are to ventilation and air sealing or to thermal bridges."

Apart from market days, the Rue du Fort breathes that down-trodden air found in certain corners of Brussels in search of identity: metal shutters down, shops for let, empty shop windows, weary passers-by. As part of its Alsemberg-Parc neighbourhood contract, the municipality of Saint Gilles wants to set up what could be called a "citizen boulevard". In this context, the run-down building right next to the former Gunther Piano factory – which the Flemish Community has now turned into the *De Pianofabriek* cultural centre – was targeted for refurbishment. The plan here was to turn the bottom floor into an environmental advisory centre, while the upper floors were to be converted into a three-floor maisonette, which would be rented out by the Régie Foncière as owner.

There is thus a dual example here: that of an exemplary (Batex) refurbishment project with regard to Brussels targets in this fields, and that of a template for local residents wanting to invest, at their own speed, in an upcoming area. This was behind the designers' clear-cut wish to "stick to simple building techniques and materials easy for local residents to use in any low-key refurbishment project – whether with regard to the budget available or energy-saving targets." The tone is set – in line with local realities.

This realism is first and foremost a self-imposed constraint. In terms of energy performance, insulation and airtightness have been done with the greatest care, using the most suitable methods while preserving as much as possible of the house's main structure and without trying to squeeze the last drop out of available energy-saving measures. The new wood-framed building at the bottom of the garden, built between two existing terraced houses, will not meet the originally intended passive criteria, as the neighbouring building robs it of the necessary sunlight.

Architect Cédric Polet: "We might have been able to have managed it by putting in fifty centimetres or more of insulation. Or by cheating on the living area via the inclusion of a mezzanine to artificially boost the PHPP calculations. But for what? Our aim is to demonstrate the maximum achievable under the given circumstances. There's nothing wrong in clearly defining the limits of the whole exercise."

An exercise in humility probably not without frustration for professionals with their tendency for perfection. And which can give rise to a certain amount of criticism from those saying that things need to be done urgently and that oil prices are already soaring.

The answer to this is that "it's true that the solutions here are far from being perfect. But we believe that, given the current state of mentalities in neighbourhoods such as these, it would be wrong to want to move faster than the music. We need to allow people wanting to renovate their homes to progress in the right direction at their own pace without immediately being faced with financial constraints. In this neighbourhood, at this level, when people start renovating and when they see how much the materials needed cost, they are quickly tempted to give up. We need therefore to tread carefully, step by step. If needs be by starting with the replacement of light bulbs. You just can't start talking to them about Blower Doors® and airtightness. That doesn't mean that we don't broach the subject, but we do so with ideas closer to their everyday lives. It's just a question of where one comes from and where one wants to go. And it's a long road! Getting energy consumption down from the current 150 or 160 kW/m² per year – the average for most houses in this area – to 50 or even 45 is already a major step forward." And we will probably end up at 15 – 30 kWh/m² a year. A very exemplary project – and a lesson with great scope for others7...

"It is very interesting to set a target objective . This provides the context for each and every project. One can achieve it, surpass it, or fall short for good reasons or otherwise."
Olivier Mathieu, architect

"Our first experiment back in 2007 [020] served to underline the necessity of really going through everything from start to finish when designing a project."
Project owner Michel Nederlandt

"Even before the first Batex call for projects, our approach was going in the right direction. Batex just helped us continue along the path, going into greater detail."
Architect Sebastian Moreno-Vacca

"Batex is a collective process. It's very encouraging being among the selected projects. They generate a true momentum, confirming objectives and means in the eyes of the project owners".
Architect Pierre Somers

Passive public housing on Rue Bruyn [100]: fragment of a new sustainable neighbourhood planned by the CPAS/OMCW of the Municipality of Brussels-City at Neder-Over-Heembeek; this ensemble of 79 homes is built to prevent people looking onto each other's balconies and to give more sun and privacy to the inhabitants (P. Blondel, architect) > see chapter 7.

Passive public housing on Rue passive Fineau [091]: for these three dwellings intended for the CPAS/OMCW of the Municipality of Brussels-City, the architects have drawn up a tenants' "manual" (Délices architectes).

Passive house on Rue de Vrière [044]: this is the smallest Batex house project; it is raised on stilts to preserve the garden (B. Van Leeuw and H. Van Eetvelde architects).

Renovation of the Florair social housing complex [061]: this housing block, typical of the fifties, needs to be renovated in order to divide by four the heating needs of its 183 units (P. Segui, architect).

04/ TAKING THE CITY AS IT COMES

The projects respond to a wide range of needs, to specific situations and to sometimes uneven levels of know-how. Whether a beginner or a seasoned professional, everyone has used his own means to go as far as possible.

Is there any common denominator between the 30-bed crèche built in the Rue Saint-François [071] by the municipality of Saint-Josse and the private house in the Rue du Verrewinkel in Uccle? [083] Or between the refurbishment of a house in the Avenue de Fléron [049] in Forest and the development of an Energy Office in an old building in the Rue du Fort [106] in Saint-Gilles? Or between the construction of a new house in the Rue Fineau [091] in Laeken and that of 79 apartments in the Rue Bruyn [100] in Neder-Over-Heembeek, especially when the buildings are operated by the same institution, the Brussels CPAS? Is it possible to compare the refurbishment of the Florair building [061] in Jette with its 18 000 m² and 183 social apartments with the construction of a small 106 m² house in the Rue De Vrière [044] in Laeken?

The first point all these projects have in common is that each project owner was able to build on his own knowledge to set suitable objectives within the framework suggested by Batex. The most exemplary path was certainly the one taken by the families now living in the 14 passive homes in the Espoir development in the Rue Fin [060]: a private development with institutional backing, and cooperation between the municipality and the Region – these were the ingredients for coming up with a true Brussels hybrid, a true "Zinneke".

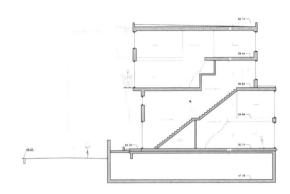

[BATEX 060 – L'ESPOIR]

Rue Fin 3-13 à 1080 Molenbeek-Saint-Jean | Fonds du Logement scrl | Damien Carnoy Architecte | MK Engineering sprl

AN EXEMPLARY CO-PRODUCTION

The Rue Fin in Molenbeek provides a terrain for urban experimentation[1], with its different public housing typologies next to each other in a non-too-salubrious area.

A modernist block of apartments built in 1975 sits next to more recent developments, built since 2004 in the context of the Fonderie-Pierron neighbourhood contract (*contrat de quartier*). At this time, the non-profit organisation Bonnevie started a cooperation project between associations and institutions[2] to enable 14 low-income families to purchase housing at a very moderate cost of construction.

WORKING IN NETWORKS

Grouped together to form the Espoir association[3], the participants compiled their programme, defining their needs and looking into a range of solutions. The Housing Fund acquired the brownfield site in Rue Fin. Their approach naturally saw them participating in the Batex call for projects.

They were set on opting for the passive standard. For Lahoussine Fadel, one of the association's founding members: "A lot of care was taken to explain to us why things should be done in a certain way, why we should be interested in a certain technical solution, and discussing with us details affecting us. We really had the impression of being involved from start to finish". Acting as prime contractor, the Housing Fund organised a design / execution competition which led to the selection of the project put forward by architect Damien Carnoy[4], himself attracted by all the work put in up-front by the future residents […] to prepare the competition document listing everybody's dreams, financial constraints, etc."

THE FIRST SUSTAINABLE 4-STOREY BUILDING MADE OF WOOD

The main building materials used were ones with a low ecological footprint, such as cellulose insulation, (FSC/PEFC) certified wood, etc. Solar cells and a "green" roof rounded off the sustainable approach for this first 4-storey building in Brussels made entirely of wood. Designed for the specific needs of each family, the lower maisonettes are accessible directly from the street on the south side. They also have small gardens behind the house. The upper maisonettes are accessible via private staircases and have large balconies. The architect responded to participants' wishes for their "houses" to be distinct from each other (each family also has its own ventilation system) in a voluntarily non-professional manner, with each one painted a different colour and avoiding shared space. The true communality of the building is to be found in the process which allowed the future neighbours to get to know each other better...

FOLLOW THE GUIDE

Living in a passive building? To dissipate any apprehensions, the architect, Bonnevie and residents have come up with a "Guide"[5] explaining the building's special constructional and technical features. This has had a snowball effect, with a number of residents now having become energy advisors and even "passive building ambassadors"[6]. In the words of Bonnevie's Donatienne Hermesse: "with an increasing number of ultra-low-energy or pas-

sive homes in our municipalities, the question is beginning to arise on how to pass on practical tips to future tenants." This pilot project holds workshops in Molenbeek where tenants of new apartments can share tips and tricks. Instead of lining the pockets of slumlords, these newcomers are now homeowners. Their repayments are securing their children's futures, at the end of an exemplary cooperation programme involving local initiatives and public and private partners.

L'Espoir is a unique project, and the whole Bonnevie framework is difficult to reproduce: the handover of the land by the municipality of Molenbeek was a great help and the Housing Fund agreed to cover the high cost of site remediation. All these conditions are basically unique. Even so, the Housing Fund's support played a decisive role in triggering and setting up the project. L'Espoir has led to new interest in collective forms of property management, as seen for instance in the Community Land Trust (CLT).

[1] Sarah Lévy, "Expérimentation in-situ", *A+* 212, June 2008, p. 39.
[2] The non-profit organisation Coordination et Initiatives pour et avec les Réfugiés et Etrangers (CIRE) and the Brussels-Capital Region Housing Fund.
[3] Read the report in *be.passive* 05, September 2010, p. 58, and the interview of the "Passive building ambassadors" (Ambassadeurs du passif) in *be.passive* 11, p. 14. See also: Thomas Dawance, "Immigrés pauvres éco-bâtisseurs", in *Alter-Echos* 258, 12.09.2008.
[4] www.carnoy-crayon.be/
[5] www.bonnevie40.be/images_th/bijlage_781_2586.pdf
[6] Caroline Chapeau, "L'Espoir: Les ambassadeurs du passif", in *be.passive* 11 June 2012, p. 12.
[7] Michel Renard, "Community Land Trust: un espoir pour le logement", *be.passive* 08, July 2011, p. 48.

COMMUNITY LAND TRUST (CLT)

The CLT is a form of communal property management, neither public nor fully private, where the property remains owned by the trust, thereby putting a cap on soaring property prices. The CLT offers the possibility of counteracting housing pressure in cities, for the benefit of private individuals and the community alike. The CLT's roots can be traced back to Great Britain and the USA. The trust is an association which owns land and buildings, managing them for the benefit of the community [7].

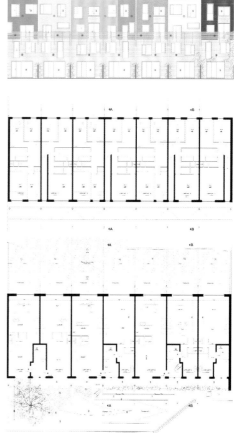

Lahoussine and Yassine Fadel,
tenants

[TESTIMONY]
AN URBAN ADVENTURE...
AND A HUMAN ONE
L'ESPOIR [060]

A few years ago they would have wryly told you that a building like this was just not up
their street. Not within their means. And now they are living there, and even owning their homes.
There are even some thinking that there's nothing exceptional about their adventure...
you just need to want it.

"When they spoke to us about low or very low energy, then about passive, we didn't believe them. Especially when they told us there would be no radiators. We said to ourselves that with winters like we have them in Belgium, it will be hell."

At those first meetings organised by Molenbeek's Bonnevie Community Centre and Le Ciré back in 2004, everyone seemed full of doubts. Though this local building project with its apartments was not without interest, for most tenant families with their low incomes, it was just out of reach. And the very thought of one day actually owning one of these comfortable apartments...

Nevertheless a dozen families accompanied the planning phase from start to finish, from meeting to meeting, drafting the plans and watching the project come into being – the purchase of the land by the Molenbeek Housing Association with the help of the municipality and the Neighbourhood Contract, the funding via the Housing Fund, project definition, the distribution of the apartments, visits to passive homes, tenders, etc.

Lahoussine Fadel attended all meetings right from the start: "We were told that, via the Housing Fund, the apartments were within our means. To start with, we couldn't really believe this, but when they started asking us about what size and layout we would like the apartments to have and to discuss kitchen arrangements, we started to catch on (Editor's note: the reason behind the name adopted by the residents' association – L'Espoir or *Hope*)... We started saving in 2006. We had a big party the day the land was purchased."

At that time, technical aspects, environmental options – the use of eco-building materials, collecting rainwater, green roofs, wooden frames, etc. – or energy performance aspects were a bit too much for most of them – "We didn't understand much. What we did grasp was that savings were going to be made in running costs – costs that at that time were costing us a fortune".

Since then, they have all made progress with the help of the Bonnevie residents' association. Léonie Pindi, Lahoussine Fadel and Mustapha Mechbal (who at the end of the day dropped out, though still taking part in the meetings) have even become "passive construction ambassadors". And now they are true believers, despite last winter which was particularly hard and which led a pragmatic Leonie to say: "In such extreme situations, there are still a few adjustments needing to be done. We need to sit down and discuss them". But there is also pride when they start talking about their new homes: "During the day when outside temperatures were down to 14 degrees below zero, temperatures in the lower floor apartments sometimes went down to 16 degrees plus, but in the evening, when the whole family was at home, we were normally back to 20 degrees..."

The general opinion is that at the end of the day it was the human adventure which welded them to this project, developed from one meeting to the next by a group consisting of eleven different nationalities and which ended in twelve local families finding a home. Lahoussine: "At the end of these six years, it is not just a home that we have gained – we have also learned how to confront different people in often difficult discussions. What we now have is one big family with twenty-four members!" Apart from the project's technical features, the name of the project, "L'Espoir", established early in the initial meetings, underlines the project's meaning.

The Rue de la Science/ Rue Belliard [142]: corner will be disengaged and the public area lined with shops and a large atrium. Heating and cooling will be covered by a system of geothermal wells. 120 geothermal mini-wells drilled to a depth of 100m at the rear of the building cover 80% of heating needs in winter (Art & Build architects).

05/ REPLIES TO THE CALL FOR PROJECTS

Together with the high number of comparable projects, there are lots of individual circumstances (such as the lack of a call for projects in 2010) preventing representative statistical processing. Here is an attempt to come up with a few figures.

WHO RESPONDED TO THE CALL?

Of the 245 projects submitted in the 4 calls, 238[1] were deemed valid. One-third of applications (76) involved apartment blocks, immediately followed by private houses (70), public amenities (53) and finally offices (39). 35% of project owners came from the public sector, 32% were private individuals, 24% were private companies and 8% non-profit organisations.

The first call was a great success. After 2009, public-sector commissions[2] and those of private individuals increased, while commercial companies remained less present. Figures for non-profit organisations increased, and they were to become, along with private individuals, the sector with more commissions in 2011 than in the first call, perhaps because small projects could now benefit from a basic grant independent of the floor space involved.

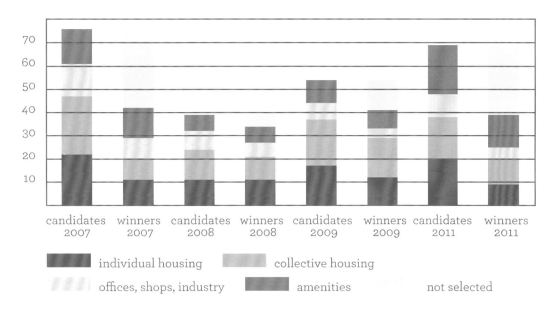

candidates 2007 — winners 2007 — candidates 2008 — winners 2008 — candidates 2009 — winners 2009 — candidates 2011 — winners 2011

individual housing collective housing offices, shops, industry amenities not selected

PROJECT OWNERS	2007	2008	2009	2011	TOTAL	
public sector	27	10	20	26	83	35 %
private individuals	22	12	19	24	77	32 %
companies	22	13	13	10	58	24 %
non-profit orgs.	5	4	2	9	20	8 %
total	76	39	54	69	238	

WHICH APPLICANTS WERE SUCCESSFUL?

The distribution of successful applicants basically mirrors that of the candidates. Comparing the last call with the previous ones, we see that the public sector share has remained stable, that of non-profit organisations is up, and that of companies down. Increasing since 2007, we saw the private housing trend dip in 2011.

The profiles of successful applicants differ in floor space terms, with a number of commercial projects larger than others. Whereas the applications of private individuals and non-profit organisations remained more or less constant, commercial projects tended to be larger yet not so numerous. We did however see a sharp rise in public-sector projects in 2011, with twice the amount of floor space as in previous years.

After three major applications from hospitals in 2007-2008, non-profit organisation projects are now smaller but more numerous, meaning that more such organisations have gained the necessary skills to submit Batex applications.

[1] Together with the 7 applications that could not be accepted, for example due to incomplete documentation, the total number of participants was 245, with some coming back year after year.
[2] The SDRB's Midi-Suède project and L'Espoir are counted as private commissions as they involved the private property market.

SUCCESSFUL APPLICATIONS	2007	2008	2009	2011	TOTAL	
public sector	18	9	18	18	63	40 %
private individuals	9	11	14	12	46	30 %
companies	12	10	7	3	32	20 %
non-profit orgs.	3	4	2	6	15	10 %
total	42	34	41	39	156	

WINNERS m²	2007	2008	2009	2011	TOTAL m²	m²	GRANTS €	
public sector	24 086	26 544	27 408	60 684	138 723	37 %	9 945 839	43 %
private individuals	1 736	2 289	3 118	1 792	8 935	2 %	925 101	4 %
companies	85 865	23 630	23 070	33 337	165 902	45 %	7 621 982	33 %
non commercial	19 681	22 939	7 314	8 431	58 365	16 %	4 758 249	20 %
total	131 368	75 402	60 909	104 245	371 924		23 251 171	

WHO ARE RECEIVING BATEX GRANTS?

Distribution is proportional to project floor space and the type of project owner, and takes into account the regulations for awarding grants with regard to their minimum and maximum amounts[1]. With the 43 projects submitted by private individuals being fairly low in price, they only took up 4% of the total EUR 24 million provisional budget. The private sector took up 33% of grants for offices, retail floor space, apartment blocks, etc.; non-profit organisations accounted for 21% for crèches, schools, hospitals, private projects, etc., while the public sector accounted for the highest percentage, taking up 42% for housing and public amenity projects.

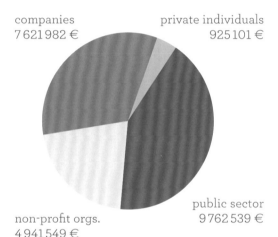

companies
7 621 982 €

private individuals
925 101 €

non-profit orgs.
4 941 549 €

public sector
9 762 539 €

Looking at all 4 calls, 58% of grants (EUR 13 million) went to the private sector. Non-profit organisations used 78% of their grants for public amenities (for the most part for hospitals in 2007-2008, but also for schools). The rest of the private sector share was divided up between commercial companies (45% for offices, 26% for apartment blocks and 12% for industrial operations) and, to a much lesser extent, private individuals (86% in private houses).

On the other hand, the mechanisms used for allocating Batex grants had the effect of putting a ceiling on grants awarded to the "big players", preventing them getting too large a slice of the cake. This resulted in the average grant per m[2] decreasing[2] as projects got bigger. This in turn allowed more participants to be covered by the same amount of grants and to constitute a critical mass.

WHAT ARE BATEX GRANTS USED FOR?

A systematic analysis shows their distribution between private commissions (including housing companies and non-profit organisations) and public ones in terms of houses, apartment blocks, offices and public amenities. Public commissions mainly targeted housing, while private ones focused mainly on offices and public amenities.

[1] The maximum grant for any one project is set at EUR 500,000 for the project owner and EUR 100,000 for the project architect; the minimum is EUR 5,000. Grants are capped at EUR 200,000 over a period of three fiscal years for project owners subject to European de minimis aid regulation, such as commercial companies, public or private organisations, non-profit organisations with business activities, etc. (Commission Regulation (EC) No 1998/2006 of 15 December 2006 on the application of Articles 87 and 88 of the Treaty to de minimis aid). Projects not selected are also given compensation.
[2] This averages 100 €/m[2] for private houses, 73 €/m[2] for apartment blocks, 69 €/m[2] for public amenities and 51 €/m[2] for offices.

DISTRIBUTION PER TYPE OF PROGRAMME AND ORDER
(millions of euros)

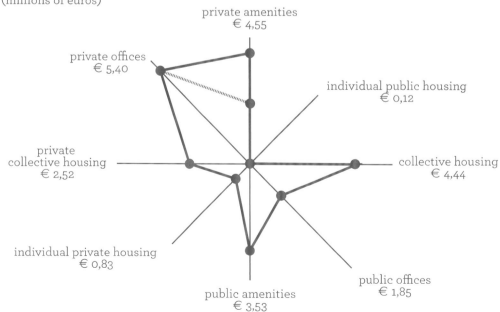

private amenities
€ 4,55

private offices
€ 5,40

individual public housing
€ 0,12

private collective housing
€ 2,52

collective housing
€ 4,44

individual private housing
€ 0,83

public offices
€ 1,85

public amenities
€ 3,53

Magasin Caméléon [025]: delivered in 2009, the Magasin Caméléon includes offices, a housing unit, a nursery and more than 12,000 m² of retail space, coiled around an atrium allowing natural ventilation and passive cooling. A pellet boiler, rainwater cistern and eco-materials complement the approach, which has also worked on the landscaping and biodiversity of the site (among other things by installing beehives on the roof) (C. Wittock architect).

Heightening of a school on Avenue Victor Rousseau in passive building [149]: the asbl Institut Sainte Ursule was a Batex winner in 2011 with a four-classroom extension on the roof of its building in Forest (Trait, Norrenberg & Somers Architectes).

Renovation of the Brasseries Belle-Vue [112]: the conversion of this impressive industrial building into a 150-room hotel complex should make it possible to guarantee a level of comfort worthy of a 4-star hotel (A2M architects).

06/ PRIVATE SECTOR MOMENTUM

Leaving aside the EUR 2 million allocated to the three major hospital projects in 2007-2008 Brugmann CHU [036] and CTR [076] and the Saint-Pierre CHU [072], the current programming applying to private amenities mainly involves healthcare infrastructures, such as the Ceriseraie [037] in Schaerbeek or the Coupole de l'autisme [110] in Jette, schools such as Immi [023] in Anderlecht, Horeca projects such as Belle-Vue [112] in Molenbeek, etc.

There are just so many stakeholders willing to consider how they can contribute to making buildings, neighbourhoods and the whole city more sustainable!

The highest grants are going towards the construction of offices and business premises. In the office sector, half of the grants were awarded in the first call for projects in 2007. 70% went into office projects such as Elia [020] in Brussels, refurbishment projects such as Mundo-B [067] in Ixelles or Loi 42 [068] in Etterbeek, or again the

Aéropolis II offices [040] in Schaerbeek. This last project, the first passive office block in Brussels, is very much representative of current discussions on a "sustainable tertiary sector" in Brussels.

For the rest, 10% of Batex grants are going into commercial projects, such as Caméléon [025] in Woluwé-Saint-Lambert or Urbanscape [013] in Uccle, and 20% into business projects such as the Mabru morning market [069] or the workshop at the Ferme Nos Pilifs [011].

[BATEX 040 – AEROPOLIS II]

Avenue Urbain Britsiers at 1030 Schaerbeek | Maison du Travail asbl | Architectes Associés | Cenergie

OFFICES COMPLYING WITH SUSTAINABLE STANDARDS

The Aéropolis II passive offices[1] were delivered in 2010 by the Agence Architectes Associés[2] for the ARCO group and the Huis van de Arbeid non-profit organisation. For the architects, what was at stake here was to come up with a template for a standard sustainable office building in line with the typical requirements of the Brussels market.

"WE OFFERED OUR CLIENTS A PASSIVE DESIGN"

The completed building differs somewhat from the project that won the private competition organised by the contractors in 2006. "We decided to evaluate the costs of a passive building, proposing this option to the client", explained architect Sabine Leribaux[3]. In the meantime, the sustainable construction virus had reached the architects, who wanted to make the Aéropolis the first major passive office block in Brussels... and this saw them participating in the Batex call for projects. The building meets the top comfort and building management criteria demanded by the European clientele, but with greatly reduced electricity and heating requirements allowing the owners to recover the additional 4% in building costs within a 5-year period.

THE FIRST PASSIVE CURTAIN-WALL

Built on a reinforced concrete frame, the building sports the first passive curtain-wall in Belgium, developed by facade specialist Belgométal. The company has developed modules whose aluminium shield is fixed onto a prefabricated structure made of FSC/PEFC certified wood, insulated by the Resol® and made completely airtight. Glass cladding on top of a neutral steel sheet gives the modules a dark grey pearl appearance, providing them with good solar properties. This ultra-high-performance shell, coupled with high airtightness, reduces heating requirements to 8 kWh/m² a year.

AVOIDING AIR CONDITIONING

Deceptively compact, the building sports a full height atrium, bringing more natural light and making it easier to ventilate the building on hot summer days. The layout is mainly open to the north and more closed to the south, a design aimed at providing comfort in the summer without the need for air-conditioning. To maximise solar gains, just 30% of the walls are glazed and the building has dispensed with false ceilings (air is circulated using false floors) to make the most of the building's thermal inertia. A dual "Canadian well" around the foot of the building contributes to passive cooling in summer. The design was seen to pay its way in the hot summer of 2010, when outside temperatures reached 31°C, in contrast to the 24°C inside! Where a conventional office building would consume 27 kWh/m² a year for cooling, Aéropolis uses a mere... 2 kWh!

MADE TO LAST

Modulation in three widths permits a composition that architect Marc Lacour defines as "random controlled". Their arrangement ensures optimal natural light conditions while allowing functional plasticity of space, thereby making possible many different layouts. Built to last, the project features environmental and constructional qualities, but also and above all spatial qualities. For Sabine Leribaux, "Being responsible, whether as an architect or a human being, cannot be subordinated to recognition. On the contrary, being awarded Batex recognition enabled us to believe that what we were doing was important and open to everyone – something we had our doubts about. This spurred us on to put all our efforts into getting there."

[1] See the Mister Emma reports on www.archiurbain.be/?p=208 and in be.passive 05, September 2010, p. 31 ff.
[2] www.architectesassocies.be
[3] Read the report in be.passive 05, September 2010, p. 31-38.

Benoît Ceysens,
promoter

ONCE THE HABIT HAS BEEN ACQUIRED
NOS PILIFS [011]

For more than twenty-five years, all projects of this sheltered company have followed the natural trend of respect for the collective heritage. This of course meant that this new building for post-production and mail-order activities on the company's five-hectare site had to be exemplary. For them it was obvious:

"We wanted a building that would blend well into the landscape. We took advantage of the slopes to half-bury the building – it is visible only from the south. Other solutions evolved as the project took shape..."

"Our social mission is to work with handicapped employees, fully respecting their dignity. Since starting up in 1984, we have always seen it as being completely natural to do this in a context respecting the environment. All our decisions revolve around the same questions: does this suit the needs of our handicapped workers? Will this end up providing them with good working conditions? Is it in line with our environmental targets?"

A garden business offering garden products, a grocery-bakery shop, a post-production workshop, a pub, a demonstration farm, everything goes in the same direction at Nos Pilifs –- as witnessed by several official awards: eco-dynamic company, winner of the Foundation for Future Generations Grand Prix.

Benoît Ceysens, head of the company, is by no means a guru or a narrow-minded militant. Nor an adventurer, even if in the late eighties he was at the origin of the largest Belgian building built of mud-and-straw: "At that time, it was a UFO. The house of the three piglets. But it was also an exciting experiment which provided us with media attention, helping us to "sell" what we do here to the outside world."

When in the early 2000's the decision needed to be taken to relocate our post-production and mail-order activities, the way do it was obvious – just do what we have always done. All that remained to be done was to find professionals sensitive to and interested in sustainable construction methods and creative and original solutions – provided they were able to convince and seduce the board, even having to justify some small overruns. "Even though we are a non-profit organisation and to a large extent dependent on sponsors, donors and government subsidies, we use professionals and remunerate them accordingly."

At that time, he acknowledged, there was not much expertise available on low-energy construction and the associated special techniques, but what they wanted was clear: "We wanted a building that would blend well into the landscape". This saw us opting for an unusual plan: "We took advantage of the slopes to half-bury the building – it is visible only from the south. Other solutions evolved as the project took shape, with the help of the architects[1] who built a mock-up of the building."

Listening to Benoît Ceysens, everything seems to be quite simple, based on proved solutions adapted to the circumstances, such as the wood chip heating system: "It was only logical that all this wooden waste, to be found in any garden centre, should, when not composted, be used for heating. Otherwise we have to pay to get rid of it..."

But at the end of the day, one has to stay realistic: "We ended up not achieving the passive standard. Despite all our efforts, we only achieved 0.8 instead of the targeted 0.6 – mainly due to the big sliding door needed for bringing in the goods. We made four attempts before giving up. But the IGBE was conciliatory..."

This said, the head of Nos Pilifs never loses sight of the effects deriving from the whole approach, in particular with regard to planting the building's roof. "This is something right up our street. And for us, it represents the future. This building is our new business card. We would like to be participating in a change of attitudes, helping this trend to gain maturity, for example by developing near-to-nature gardens and moving away from boring lawns and other barren green spaces." And slipping in a suggestion for Brussels Environment: "Following the example of exemplary (Batex) buildings, what about another quality label for 'company buildings surrounded by near-to-nature landscaping'..." Anyone listening?

[1] Matriciel

Malibran community centre and housing on Rue des Cygnes-Rue de la Digue [039]: the result of a competition In 2005, this project presents a complex architecture determined by the existing plot structure and anchored in the heart of the island. The homes "fold up" to reconcile the built volume necessary for the programme with the equally necessary empty volume of the courtyards (Lpp architects, AA0 and Label architecture).

Espoir passive homes, Rue Fin [060] (D. Carnoy, architect).

07/ PUBLIC-SECTOR MOMENTUM

The public sector is investing 46% of Batex grants in housing (606 units) and 36% in public amenities, mainly for crèches, schools and polyclinics.

Together with the non-profit sector, the public sector accounts for 63% of all Batex grants, which thereby flow back to society in the form of support for social housing, services and public amenities.

Looking at the floor space involved, we are seeing a progressive downturn on the part of the private sector, and a corresponding upturn in public-sector projects, up from 18% of total floor space in 2007 to 58% in 2011.

DISTRIBUTION BETWEEN PRIVATE AND PUBLIC SECTORS (IN AREA)

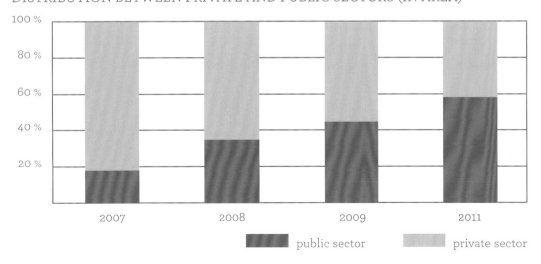

public sector   private sector

Passive homes on Rue de Suède [034]: well oriented north-south, but in a dense urban fabric, the façade reinterprets the theme of the traditional bay window and optimizes solar gains. This project was nominated for the MIPIM Awards 2012 (Urban Platform, architect).

House renovation on Rue Crocq [079]: the renewal of the roof led to the raising of the attic, creating a large window and increasing the living space while improving the flow of natural light (FHW architect).

08/ TOWARDS A LESS PRECARIOUS URBANITY?

Though private and public players are interested in Batex for different reasons, at the end of the day, their different motivations mirror the momentum and paradoxes found within Brussels. A large number of Batex projects are located in areas where major urban renewal work is already in progress... but not always for the same reasons.

The private sector and especially the office sector – the sector hardest hit by the crisis – are in two minds about which sustainable office model needs to be developed "to make the difference" in a highly competitive market and to define the architectural side of the new "corporate social responsibility"[1] where environmental scores are gaining in weight. Yet such players remain the exception in their sector.

The public-sector players are looking for robust solutions aimed at keeping households in the city and fighting the (in particular energy-related) precariousness of council tenants. They are often faced with the task of developing brownfield sites, where environmental pollution needs to be taken into account. To attract and retain families, they need to provide housing and infrastructures in an easy-to-live-in quality. Batex provides them with the opportunity of creating a consistent "short loop" between their projects and other public funding, as they often find themselves competing with private players.

[1] Voir Jean-Marc Gollier, "La profession libérale, une profession comme une autre ?", be.passive 11, June 2012.

IN THE WORDS
OF A PROJECT OWNER

"Fortunately the pioneers are often very communicative, taking time to provide guidance. Moreover, a number of entrepreneurs are getting to know each other and work together on exemplary sites, before regrouping to work in other cooperation projects – a very positive development."

Olivier Alexandre

"Coaching specialised services acts as a watchdog. Even if we have the luck to find an architect with a good command of this type of project, an interested entrepreneur, attentive and very motivated in adding this reference to his list of achievements..."

Benoît Ceysens

09/ LEARNING PROFESSIONALS

The response of Brussels citizens to the call for projects surpassed all expectations. "For Brussels, the call for projects has meant putting the foot down on the accelerator", said Grégoire Clerfayt [1].

With sustainability in the news [2], architects, companies and contractors were already engaged in training in passive building methods, sustainable construction and energy management back in 2007, and Brussels Environment, the Construction Confederation and Passive Platforms were introducing training and information schemes [3].

Though constructing or refurbishing an "exemplary" building is obviously no easy task, one is not completely alone. Names circulate from one project to the next, as well as addresses of suppliers, specialists and specialised manufacturers. And during the building work, the authorities do not leave the applicants out in the rain. "Batex support to project owners is very valuable, involving making experience available to everyone, for the benefit of everyone..." explained architect and project owner Olivier Alexandre, Rue Huberti [051]. Batex has also prepared the ground for monitoring the energy consumption of the projects over a 5-year period and regularly sends out technical notes summarising feedback from successful applicants [4].

At the end of the day, it is the commitment of the investing project owners, coupled with the creativity and competence of the design teams, architects and engineers, which makes all the difference: "we have lots of extremely well-trained architects and engineers... but they don't know it!" commented Grégoire Clerfayt [5]. Moving from zero passive building in 2007 to more than 40 000 m² in 2009 [6], not to mention the refurbished buildings which also go extremely far – all this has been done on the basis of our existing knowledge, some locals and without any major training campaigns, etc. This all demonstrates the market's ability to do the extraordinary!"

Batex has opened up a transitional forum. For engineer Bram De Meester, "The exemplary buildings have triggered a dialogue in the sector between the public authorities, project owners and designers / architects. Stakeholders now know about sustainability concepts, which themselves are now available in greater detail." On the one hand, Batex is showing the "transitions" able to be accomplished in the face of the dual imperative of climate change and the disappearance of cheap oil [7]: Batex is an instrument allowing progress to be made.

On the other hand, Batex is a forum where everyone may, progressively and based on his own situation, learn about new techniques and new demands through checking them with reality and with experts: Batex is a new learning forum.

---

[1] From Brussels Environmental Department for Energy, Air, Climate and Sustainable Building.
[2] 2007 saw Al Gore's film, the fourth IPCC report, the Stern report, petrol prices shooting up, etc.
[3] See tools, information material, info leaflets p. 228-229.
[4] See tools, information material, technical files on exemplary buildings, p. 229.
[5] In be.passive 02, 2010, www.bepassive.be
[6] Editors' note: 145 000 m² in 2011.
[7] In the full sense of the Cities in Transition movement, www.transitionnetwork.org; www.entransition.be

House renovation on Rue Traversière [084]: this project includes a planted façade, a tour de force that brings a touch of greenery into a narrow and very "mineral" street (atelier d'architecture Matz-Haucotte).

IN THE WORDS OF THE EXPERTS

"It is a great opportunity for furthering discussions and we intend to share this experience."
Architect Sébastien Cruyt

"The main positive impact is with staff. You can't imagine how proud staff were in having to learn a new trade for the project in Molenbeek [060], and in successfully constructing a four-storey wooden frame."
Entrepreneur Olivier Mareschal

"After four rounds of Batex, I still find the approach and the open source spirit as convincing as at the start."
Architect Gérard Bedoret

Passive social housing on Avenue Dubrucq [018]: this project combines a traditional reinforced concrete frame with an envelope of prefabricated wood caissons, insulated and secured from the outside (B-architecten).

SUSTAINABLE CONSTRUCTION
PROVIDING IT WITH A FRAMEWORK AND OPENING IT UP

CHAPTER 02

Everyone understands that no building project is born of an energy bill
— it is born of a desire to live, translated into a life plan in an architectural
form. Once it has been born, the questions of technical and financial
resources arise. And slowly — through the use of common sense rules
— the project gains shape and materialises. The building needs to be stable,
lying solidly on its foundations, and dry. This is the famous "ten-year
guarantee" which appeared in the nineteenth century with the Civil Code.
Nowadays, new ethical requirements are gradually emerging, based
on observations of the impacts buildings have on the environment and public
health, and their operating costs. Batex provides four main thrusts
for sustainable construction.

Passive homes in Harenberg [136]: this eco-neighbourhood project will provide 30 passive housing units (including 5 zero energy) with ecological waste water treatment. The prefabrication in reinforced concrete will reduce costs (A2M architects).

01/ SETTING THE KEY POINTS

These new social expectations mean action - on the energy front, a building should consume hardly any energy; on the health front, a building should contribute to the health and well-being of its inhabitants; and on the environmental front, a building should contribute to better mobility, to greater biodiversity, to enhancing a natural urban landscape, etc.

Even with Batex stressing the importance of a project's energy and sustainable construction features, we need to stop underestimating them. "Practically zero-energy" and "practically zero footprint" are new features, complementing the requirements for stability and watertightness. Batex is not defining a new form of architecture, but a roadmap for today's architects in which these four criteria each have the same importance.

It is important to set ambitious targets, since the property sector only adapts slowly to change. This is why Batex has selected the sector's best practices to set its scope of action. In the words of Grégoire Clerfayt, "In 2007, we did not really know what to expect. We had not set any minimum performance standard. All we had defined were a course, targets and objectives." These objectives will evolve as we move forwards with the Batex calls, in line with the successful projects and advances in the sector.

It's up to Brussels citizens to come up with new forms of building taking their ecological consequences into account. It's up to them to define the best possible environmental and energy footprint for their projects. And finally, it's up to them to select the means best suited to achieving their objectives.

BUILDINGS ARE
RESPONSIBLE FOR 72%
OF BRUSSELS' EMISSIONS

The Brussels-Capital Region has a
non-typical profile, with 72% of its
CO_2 emissions coming from
buildings (compared with the
European average of 40%). 41% are
attributable to the residential sector
and 31% to the tertiary sector. With
industry practically non-existent
(4%), transportation is responsible
for the rest (23%). Since 2004, energy
consumption in Brussels has
dropped 17% despite population
growth, and GHG emissions have
also gone down 12%.

02/ KEY POINT 1: TO BE AS EFFECTIVE AS POSSIBLE ON THE ENERGY FRONT

A Batex project tends towards "zero energy", in line with the motto that the best energy is always that which we don't consume. To get there, designers / architects are inspired by the "energy triad" principle: reducing energy needs, using renewable energy sources and adopting the most efficient technologies.

Thermal insulation, airtightness, solar gains and energy recovery reduce the need for energy for heating in winter; bioclimatic strategies limit or eliminate the need for cooling in summer.

Batex sets indicative targets to be interpreted in the context of each project, i.e. a net heating need of ≤ 30 kWh / m² per year for refurbishment projects (20% of the building's current consumption) or ≤ 15 kWh / m² year (passive standard) for new buildings[1].

Other energy needs (for hot water, lighting, etc.) can also be targeted for reduction in the design phase and covered by the use of renewable energy sources. For anything remaining, fossil-based energy is used, with technical facilities as efficient as possible.
To achieve "zero energy", the project must go further, fully eliminating energy consumption[2]. There are two ways possible: using renewable energy (such as rapeseed oil or pellets) and / or directly captured energy (solar, wind, etc.), or investing in schemes supporting renewable energy sources to compensate for one's own CO_2 emissions.

THE PASSIVE STANDARD: A BASE FRAMEWORK

This is an effective technical and scientific framework for reducing the heating energy needs of buildings while at the same time improving their comfort. And it has been verified in tens of thousands of implementations throughout Europe. The Brussels-Capital Region has defined precise criteria for certifying buildings as passive, and calculations need to be done using the PHPP software[3].

The obligation for the result to comply with the standard has helped bring order to the market and clarify the expectations of project owners and the public at large. The passive standard is also shaking up the habits and convictions of professionals. The fact that it is a very demanding standard explains why certain designers / architects are critical of it becoming mandatory for all new buildings from 2015 onwards.

Batex is proposing the passive standard as the best energy choice "by default" – any other even more interesting alternative is welcome, insofar as it can be verified. The Rue Vandernoot [125] project was selected for its proposal to build a house made of straw and hemp concrete offering an alternative to the passive standard. This way of building enables the average comfort temperature to be reduced to 18 °C without any mechanical ventilation. The building's experimental character won over the selection panel. Its development could possibly open up other avenues.

We should remember that the legitimacy of all professional practice lies in its ability to respond to collective expectations – in this case this involves working towards zero energy – without preventing users from living a free life in solidarity with society.

[1] The energy objectives have also evolved in line with the results achieved in previous Batex rounds.
[2] In the context of the 2012 call for projects, the only primary energy needs considered are those for heating, hot water, auxiliary electricity (for ventilation, circulation pumps, etc.), cooling and lighting, calculated under normal circumstances using the Vade Mecum PHPP.
[3] Calculation sheet for establishing a project's energy balance (Passivhaus Projektierungs Paket or PHPP).

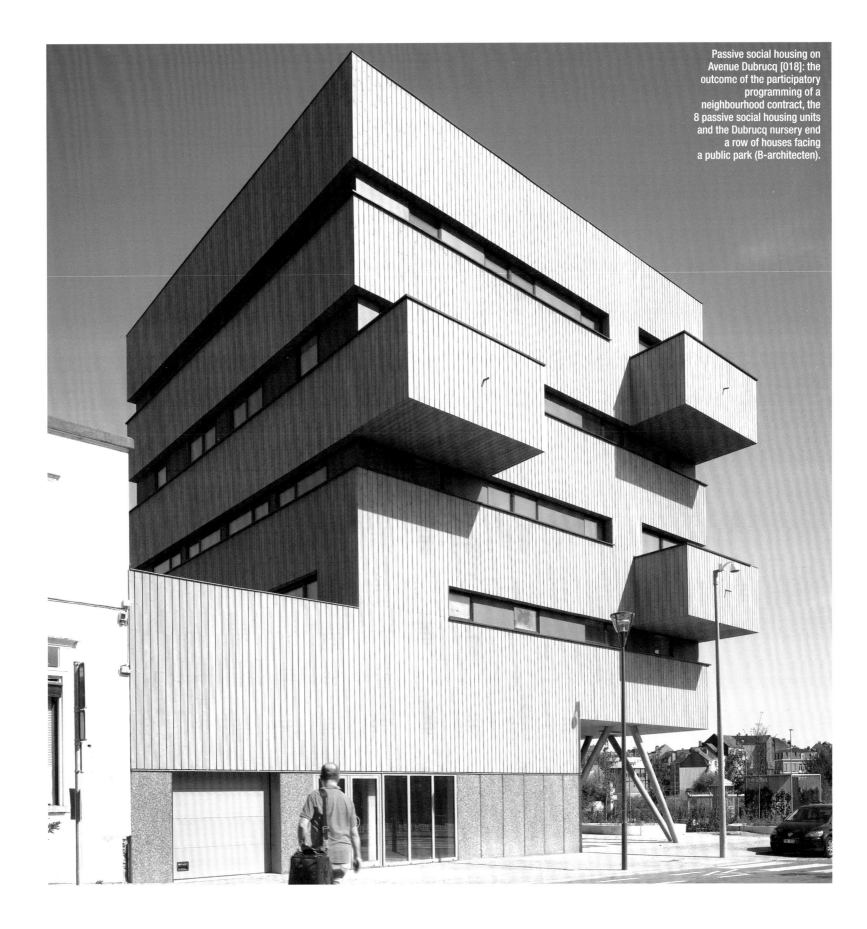

Passive social housing on Avenue Dubrucq [018]: the outcome of the participatory programming of a neighbourhood contract, the 8 passive social housing units and the Dubrucq nursery end a row of houses facing a public park (B-architecten).

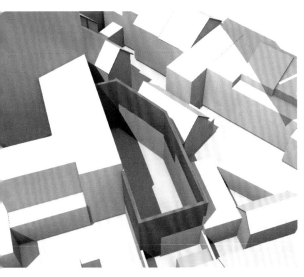

House inside the Rue de la Senne island [124]: the Senne 55 project is rebuilding a housing unit on the ruins of a workshop. Its elegant and relaxed volume stems from the study of available sunlight and of building regulations governing straight and oblique views (AAC, A. Sellier architect).

ZERO ENERGY WHILE STILL CONNECTED TO THE GRID

Zero energy in urban areas remains a gamble. We need to avoid technical one-upmanship. A city like Brussels will always be dependent on other regions for its supplies, as for its energy. "Zero energy" remains relative, especially because it is only economically viable when based at least in part on an energy grid. This allows more power to be produced in the summer and relies on the grid in the winter, when there is insufficient ambient energy. Looked at over the whole year, the balance is thus zero.

ENERGY IN AN OVERALL VISION

In Brussels, heating represents 69% of the total energy consumption of buildings. Encouraging the greatest energy efficiency possible in the building sector is therefore a crucial lever for action in Brussels, with its impact benefiting both the environment and users. But it only makes sense in the context of an overall vision of sustainable resource management combining environmental aspects with building, health, social and economic developments – i.e. the sustainable city. This is all the more important given the fact that the population of Brussels is growing: by 2020 the forecast is for a further 150 000 inhabitants, all needing housing, mobility and public amenities. It is this overall context that is pushing Brussels politicians towards sustainable construction and greater energy efficiency.

Looking at Batex projects overall, these have reduced their overall energy consumption by 80% – in refurbished buildings compared with the previous state, in new buildings compared with current regulatory requirements. Nine out of ten homes have been planned in accordance with the passive standard. More than 11 000 m² of solar collectors complement the passive strategies.

Since 2007, several projects have achieved the zero energy objective, including the social apartments in the Rue Loossens [016] and the 16 private Globe apartments [031]; others will be following in the near future, such as at Harenberg [136], or achieving near-zero energy, such as in the Rue du Biplan [055], Rue Fineau [091], Avenue des Familles [133] or the Monnoyer office block [141] or the Arts & Métiers school [154].

[BATEX 016 – RUE LOOSSENS]

Rue Loossens 42 at 1090 Jette | Foyer Jettois | A2M sprl | Ecorce

"ZERO ENERGY COST" SOCIAL HOUSING

The Foyer Jettois was selected for two flagship projects: the refurbishment of the Florair [061] apartment block and the construction of two innovative maisonettes – not just passive, but also zero-energy and zero-carbon.

This is not just a case of hoisting the "green" flag, but also underlines the major problem of rampant energy precariousness: "As a public housing company, we are looking for ways to improve our service to tenants, offering them comfortable accommodation with substantial energy savings[1]", explained Le Foyer in 2009[2]. "This has become a priority for us, as costs have now become very high, often reaching the same level as the rent itself." These apartments were completed in 2011.

(ALMOST) CONVENTIONAL CONSTRUCTION

For architect Sebastian Moreno-Vacca, it was a major challenge – the building on the three-sided plot of land was going to be small and relatively expensive. To minimize additional costs, he used conventional massive load-bearing walls, insulated with graphite-enhanced polystyrene and finished with a coating. On the ground floor a brick facing protects the construction. Less conventional is the thickness of the insulation applied to the shell – 40 cm – without any reduction of the living space in the apartments.

As a further way of limiting costs, there is only outside access to the apartments, via a side passage made necessary by the layout of the plot. Tenants can get straight to their apartments – and there is no staircase needing to be heated.

FOR LARGE APARTMENTS

Each 142 m² maisonette has 4 bedrooms. The technical core is located in the middle, enabling better sanitary ventilation and freeing up the east-facing facade. Each bedroom has one or two south-facing windows (large outside wooden shutters provide protection in the summer). The larger living rooms are on the north side.

SHARED ROOFS

To achieve zero energy, the building is first of all passive. Additional heating is distributed via a thermal battery placed in the ventilation. The building's roof captures all the energy needed to compensate for its electricity consumption and for hot water. The architect has installed 20 m² of thermal collectors (covering 60% of needs) and taken over the neighbouring roof for an additional 140 m² of photovoltaic panels – the two buildings share the electricity harvest. Even water costs are reduced, thanks to the installation of a rainwater cistern. The additional cost is expected to be amortised over 23 years by the Foyer Jettois (less if energy prices continue to rise at the current rate).

THE FIRST WINTER, THE FIRST ADJUSTMENTS

The first winter saw a regulation problem resolved. Concerned about maintaining control over the technical installation, the Foyer Jettois chose a system of regulation that gave tenants no control. Unfortunately, the system's parameters had not been checked before the winter... and tenants found it a little cold when the outside temperature dropped to -15° C! Fortunately, it was a passive apartment and the insulation allowed an acceptable temperature to be maintained. A small heater was all that was needed to solve the problem temporarily before the system parameters were adjusted.

---

[1] Via its "cost of occupation" concept, the Region would like to see half of any cost savings flowing back to the tenants in question and half to the other tenants, via the social housing companies.
[2] Vert Bruxelles! Architectures à suivre, Racine, 2009, p. 18.

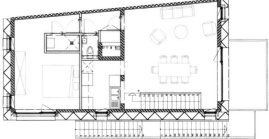

3rd floor

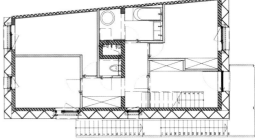

2nd floor

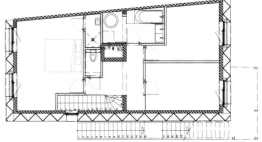

1st floor

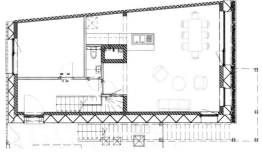

ground floor

SUSTAINABLE
CONSTRUCTION ASPECTS

1/ Neighbourhood
All of the building's and plot's amenities are designed to encourage socialising, soft mobility and biodiversity and are aimed at enhancing the urban landscape.

2/ Water
All ways of rationalising the use of water, recycling and managing rainwater are included.

3/ Materials
All measures have been taken to optimise material flows throughout the building's lifetime – on-site recycling of demolition materials, opting for new "green" materials, waste management, etc. – and to conserve natural resources.

4/ Comfort and health
All means of helping the building to meet demands regarding comfort and health and to provide a new living experience are implemented.

03/ KEY POINT 2: MINIMISING AS FAR AS POSSIBLE THE ENVIRONMENTAL IMPACT

Batex projects minimise their footprint on the environment and on occupants, with several aspects being taken into account: the choice of renewable building materials, water and waste management, biodiversity, mobility issues, the location or the use of the building in line with the surrounding urban context, etc

In this regard, candidates have at their disposal a whole range of information materials compiled by Brussels Environment[1].

Eco design relates mainly to the choice of building materials, often guided by the short loop principle, with preference being given to local materials, and making on-site (re-)use of water and waste. This involves for instance working on rainwater systems, or on reusing production waste.

[1] See Tools, info leaflets for professionals, p. 228.
[2] For households and schools, see www.bruxellesenvironnement.be
[3] See www.bruxellesenvironnement.be, Accueil > Professionnels > Themes > Energie > Maîtriser la consommation dans les bâtiments > P.L.A.G.E.
[4] See Tools, Leaflets for professionals, p. 228.

Public housing passive on Rue de la Poste [087]: the reconstruction of the housing unit on Rue de la Poste has been done with a wood frame in order to reuse the existing building foundation (CMDN architecture).

THE REGION AT THE SERVICE OF SUSTAINABLE CONSTRUCTION AND THE SUSTAINABLE CITY

Brussels Environment has come up with a whole range of incentives for encouraging energy efficiency when refurbishing existing buildings or building new ones. Several other tools have been introduced to help energy management (the energy challenge[2], social guidance , P.L.A.G.E.[3]), for promoting sustainable construction (Practical Guide[4]), for urban renewal (*Contrats de Quartiers Durables* / Sustainable Neighbourhood Contracts), the emergence of sustainable neighbourhoods, the introduction of sustainable canteens, etc

Brussels Environment has also set up a "sustainable building facilitator service", providing professionals with state-of-the-art advice on sustainable design, with a special focus on office and apartment blocks, large-size technical systems (co-generation, photovoltaic systems, solar heating, etc.), on new construction techniques and for sustainable neighbourhoods. An explanatory brochure is available on www.bruxellesenvironnement.be or www.villedurable.be

Espoir passive housing, Rue Fin [060]: the building is constructed entirely of wood (D. Carnoy, architect).

Public housing, Savonnerie Heymans [042]: the steel frame of the old soap factory was stripped bare to allow the construction of a new insulated shell (MDW architectes).

House on Rue Montagne Saint-Job [021]: many hybrid solutions are also possible, when a solid party wall is linked to a lightweight façade (G. Bedoret, architect) > see chapter 4.

04/ KEY POINT 3: ENABLING TECHNICAL AND FINANCIAL REPRODUCIBILITY

Batex projects should be simple, allowing them to be easily copied in Brussels and with a foreseeable return on investment. Environmental efficiency is assessed from the perspective of environmental benefits.

The projects focus on simple solutions which gain their bio-climatic efficiency from the building materials used rather than from technology. It is not the aim of Batex to promote technological prowess.

Financial viability is looked at via a cost-benefit analysis of the project. The price only has meaning in exchange for what it enables – well-being, operational savings, etc. The Batex objectives can be considered as investments allowing savings in operational costs and a profit after amortisation. These "additional costs" are thus always recovered within a few years. This is of interest to everyone, and especially institutional, private and public-sector players

REVISITING CONVENTIONAL WAYS OF BUILDING

The construction found in Batex projects is for the most part based on well-known building techniques. The buildings mainly selected by Batex involve conventional massive buildings, insulated, with either a concrete frame enclosed by a wooden insulating shell or an integrated wooden frame.

1/ The conventional massive construction allows airtightness to be achieved via the ceilings within the building. Insulation is applied to the outside walls, either with insulation panels finished with some form of coating, or by prefabricated insulated wooden caissons protected by cladding (wood, panels, etc.).

2/ The skeleton system allows the construction of a conventional structure in concrete enclosed in a shell of wood; airtightness is achieved through adhesive membranes, and the heavy structure needs to be perfectly connected to the lightweight elements.

3/ In an all-wood structure, use is made everywhere of products derived from wood (beams, insulation material, etc.). In such buildings, airtightness is achieved through the use of adhesive membranes. As in any construction, particular attention needs to be attached to the acoustics to avoid sound transmission. Even more attention has to be paid when the structure is made of wood[1].

4/ A number of hybrid solutions are also possible, when for instance a neighbouring wall is linked to a lightweight facade. And there are also non-typical solutions, such as insulated concrete forms, which can be suitable for private houses.

Estimates of what exemplary (Batex) buildings cost are mentioned in the technical info-sheets available on Brussels Environment's website. They vary greatly, from 359 to 1,640 €/m² for refurbishment, and from 900 to 2,170 €/m² for new buildings[2]. These amounts include measures associated with special Batex features, but also with choices specific to individual circumstances, or with the planning or the architecture of the projects in question.

Any construction or refurbishment project, whether Batex or not, is a fight against (additional) costs – additional costs[3] for building materials (more insulation, triple glazing, etc.) and false additional costs associated with the evolution of building site practices (airtightness, controls and supervision, etc.). Also not to be forgotten are design overheads (energy optimisation, comfort studies, the search for alternatives, etc.), often poorly remunerated in small projects.

[1] Damien Carnoy, David Dardenne and Luc Delvaux, "Construction bois : acoustique et/ou stabilité", in be.passive 06, January 2011, p. 72.
[2] These prices do not include VAT and architects' fees.
[3] See the interview with the architect Vincent Szpirer, be.passive 09, October 2011, p. 52-53.

IN THE WORDS OF A PROJECT OWNER

"It was a triple gamble – and we won! It involved conserving and improving a beautiful property in the Rue de la Loi, refurbishing it in a financially viable and comfortable manner without installing air-conditioning, and finally justifying the construction of new housing in the Rue de la Loi."
Eric De Keuleneer, project owner of Rue de la Loi 42 [068]

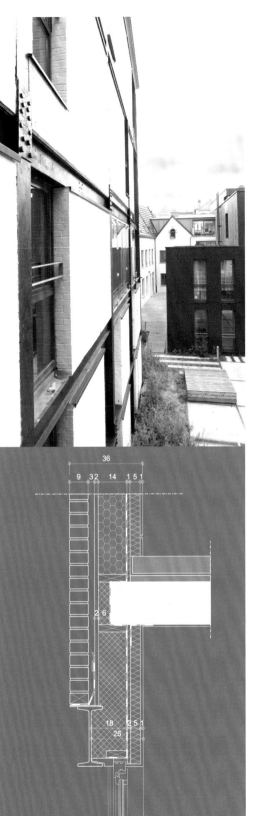

Mixed project in Chaussée de Waterloo [013]: the project combines housing and retail premises: o former car park becomes a courtyard surrounded by gardens and orchards; for this, it reorients the housing units to ensure both quality lighting and privacy for each unit (B612 architects).

Passive homes on Rue de Suède [034]: in the case of a concrete frame closed by wooden caissons, airtightness is achieved by adhesive membranes and the heavy structure must be perfectly connected to the light elements (Urban Platform Architects).

IN THE WORDS OF A COMPANY

"There are always several construction solutions available. We have worked in wood and with conventional methods. The passive standard has not changed anything. Using the passive standard does not mean that there are not several construction choices available. The main thing is to achieve the right insulation and airtightness",

Dherte's, Alain Demol

IN THE WORDS OF ARCHITECTS

"Design costs can constitute a brake."
Pierre Somers

"Whatever the budget, architectural (and environmental) quality must be forthcoming. Batex has enabled us to demonstrate this."
Sabine Leribaux

"The costs involved make it necessary to keep a close eye on estimates and project budgets to avoid ending up in an embarrassing situation and allocating blame."
Vincent Szpirer

"When out of the ordinary costs quickly become standard, somebody must be priming the pump."
Gilles Debrun

"The 'exemplary' overheads of our Batex projects (if there actually are any, as all our projects are passive ones anyhow) are amply soaked up by the grant."
Sebastian Moreno-Vacca

"We did not have any overheads actually attributable to Batex. With regard to the additional cost attributable to the passive standard [141], we are convinced that this is a question of the market, and not any real additional cost."
Sabine Leribaux

Social housing on Rue de la Brasserie [063]: the 12 housing units break down into 9 units in a main building overlooking the street, where the large south-facing balconies are freely inspired by the neighbouring Art Nouveau, and 3 homes on the site of former workshops behind the street. The project combines a concrete frame with insulated timber caissons, finished with a brick fronting (R²D² architectes).

05/ KEY POINT 4: DELIVERING ARCHITECTURAL AND URBAN QUALITY

The Batex project enriches Brussels by providing the best possible architectural quality and the best possible urban integration while taking account of its usefulness and value for the city's heritage.
Also assessed are a project's visibility and its demonstrative character.

The projects offer a wide range of innovatory solutions where environmental and technical methods are combined and formalised by the architecture: the site induces a construction- or energy-related response, technologies influence the choice of materials or implantation, etc. Questions regarding energy, technologies or savings cannot be treated separately from architectural questions.

For some years now, successful Batex applicants have been winning prizes and awards. This is the case with the Rue Wauters [017] maisonette designed by Inès Camacho, the refurbishment of the Savonnerie Heymans social apartments [042] by MDW Architectes, the passive social housing in the Rue de la Brasserie [063] designed by R²D² Architects, etc. Other projects have been nominated and the Batex operation itself was nominated in 2011 for the Belgian Energy and

Environment Prize and in 2012 for the Sustainable Energy Europe Awards.

THE SELECTION PANEL

Once submitted, the applications are examined by a panel of experts – architects, engineers, design offices specialised in sustainable construction[1] – responsible for checking a project's consistency. A selection panel[2] then selects the projects to be promoted, with the Region validating the selection.

Batex is evolving within a rapidly changing scientific, technological and regulatory environment. Though the issues of a building's stability and watertightness are well known, though new energy standards are clearly defined, other variables remain subject to debate in the fields of the choice of materials (several competing standards exist), systemic impacts on the city,

financial arrangements, the effectiveness of certain technologies, architectural quality, etc. Selection panel discussions can be long and sometimes even stormy, with a project's technical appreciation getting mixed up with regulatory, planning or architectural aspects which may be quite divergent.

The technical follow-up of projects is done by Brussels Environment, which also helps find the best solutions to the various problems cropping up at the actual building site and checking that the completed building corresponds properly to the environmental targets of the initial project.

[1] The design offices which participated in previous Batex panels (from 2007 to 2011) are Cenergie, Ingenium, Grontmij, 3E, Platform, Ecorce, Matriciel, Beco, Ageco and IPS.
[2] Other panel participants (from 2007 to 2011) include Antoine Crahay, Grégoire Clerfayt, Ismaël Daoud and Julie Goffard (for the Regional Government); Joke Dockx and Vincent Carton (for Brussels Environment); Pierre Blondel, Bernard Deprez, Dag Boutsen, Pierre Vanderstraeten, Benoît Moritz, Julien Desmet, Olivier Bastin and Thierry Decuypere (as architects); Benoît Thielemans, Pierre Hermoye, Liesbet Temmerman, Philippe Deplasse et Gauthier Keutgen (as experts).

Mathias Vandenbulcke,
architect

[TESTIMONY]

THE INGENIOUS LUCUBRATIONS OF MATHIAS "BULKY" RUE VANDENBRANDEN [118]

No risk, no innovation. In this respect, in terms of architectural concepts, this project goes the whole hog. When its architect starts talking about it, his eyes light up and he smiles like a child who loves playing tricks on adults. His project is to match. Let's hope it gets finished quickly!

"If we architects don't first test out for ourselves the original solutions that we dream up, how can we propose them to our customers?"

In the automotive sector, one would call it a "concept car". According to Wikipedia, a concept car is a one produced in very small numbers in order to showcase new styling and / or new technology. In his design studio with its touch of Zinneke Parade, Mathias Vandenbulcke (Bulky for short), architect of this astonishing project, followed the same approach. And he really enjoyed doing it... all the more so when he designated himself as the target of his ingenious lucubrations.

Several years ago, he purchased the top floor of an apartment building just a stone's throw away from the canal. And he decided to pull everything down and build two floors to his own design.

His ideas flirt with the structure of biomorphic blobs. A whole new shell is planned, keeping to the size prescribed by urban planning regulations, but with a "personal" shape and profile reminiscent of Gaudi. For the frame, he has drawn his inspiration from a structure conceived by the Dutch artist, Rinus Roelofs.

Playing with a construction allowing more morphological phantasy than a conventional roof, but also simplifying insulation and airtightness work. The wooden structural elements, designed and cut using CAD/CAM technology, require no scaffolding and can be assembled quickly with the help of a few friends. For the covering and the insulation, a reinforced concrete topping, a layer of wood wool insulation and a moisture-resistant EPDM membrane are used.

But that is only the start. On top of this construction, a unique green roof is planned – a moss "mattress" clinging on to the external membrane. Bulky explained to us that this form of "greening" has the twin virtues of not having to take root...

and filtering the fine particles released into the atmosphere by passing traffic. Its use has been tested alongside German motorways and has provided excellent results. He will be experimenting with it on the north side of the roof and in the shaded parts in the south, looking for ways of stopping it getting too dry.

For the rest, the traditional virtues of green roofs will apply: retaining rainwater, biodiversity and aesthetics. It's no use asking him whether the greenery will last for years – all you get is a candid smile: "We're still in the test phase".

Is there any need to go on and speak about the low-temperature (20°C) capillary heating system, made up of a system of micro-tubes (less than 4,3 mm diameter) integrated into a carpet that only needed to be rolled out in places where the inhabitants want just a bit more comfort?

All of this, he assured us, will work perfectly, even if you can't find anything about it in the manuals and even if it seems somewhat "borderline" in the eyes of urban planning officials. But there's nothing prohibiting it in planning regulations. "I'm quite an obedient and disciplined sort of person", he said with a disarming smile. But he intends to defend his freedom to think differently and to help urban planning advance wherever he can in the sense of history. "Sometimes it's my opinion against theirs. But it's up to me to keep my projects on the right track. It's my responsibility as an architect – and it's a responsibility I willingly assume." And for once, he looked serious...

"OK, we'll see", seemed to be one of his pet answers when doubts were uttered about the solutions he was proposing.

Redeployment on Avenue Zénobe Gramme [128]: this project to convert a former industrial building is located on a corner formed by two streets, one 3 floors lower than the other. The ensemble is being renovated to accommodate 17 passive homes and offices (Arcature scrl architects).

Nursery on Rue Kessels [117]: this project is installing a nursery with 48 places in a completely renovated ensemble of 40 intergenerational housing units; the concreted areas that used to cover the site have been replaced by gardens (GL – Shape Architecture).

BIOCLIMATIC STANDARDS FOR A DENSELY POPULATED CITY

Brussels is a region already well built-up. Opportunities for expansion or growth are mainly qualitative and involve the compactness or the mix of buildings.

The first great architectural adventure with regard to the selected projects is always their encounter – a radically bioclimatic one – with the site, taking an ecosystemic and site-specific approach. The sites and land still available are difficult to turn into housing: slopes, corners, inner courts, already densely populated areas, areas close to railway lines, brownfield sites, etc. Due to the demanding nature of the sites, the architecture is often experimental.

Certain innovatory elements of the Savonnerie Heymans project [042], such as the bioclimatic loggias, were subjected to in-depth studies and tests to deal with all usage constraints. "These indispensable updates of the construction process obviously had an impact on deadlines – but without them, you won't get any innovation", said architect Gilles Debrun. The Rue Vandenbranden extension project [118] involves an innovative and very plastic structure with a glulam frame

Batex projects demonstrate that a different bioclimatic profile, more urban, is possible. The profile is adapted to the complex situations found in a densely populated city, making the most of available light, shutting out noise, and creating privacy. A profile may expand or wriggle in search of a space of its own. Or when physical laws respond to social rules...

Insulation, triple glazing and mechanical ventilation: using an energy-saving shell, the design can make the most of the available sun, while at the same time providing protection from noise or a lack of privacy. Energy efficiency ensures usage comfort and a form of urban efficiency, especially as the designers now have available the simulation tools needed to deal with such issues as heat, light or sound, but also those of views, access, etc..

SAVINGS THROUGH POOLING

The city is based on the principle of pooling available resources. But the consumer society is changing the game, asking everyone to have their own resources. Getting back to pooling space and facilities seems to be a radically urban innovation saving space and materials and creating social coherence.

Such pooling can also apply to technical facilities, for instance when several buildings share a hea-ting system. Pooling can also involve services, such as at Mundo-B [067], where the reception, meeting rooms, etc. are shared, or at Kessels [117] where a crèche belongs to the residential development, or the provision of multi-purpose premises for the neighbourhood, as seen in the refurbishment of the Vierwinden school [150] in Molenbeek. Several projects pool space, ranging from room-sharing to co-housing[1]. Privately developed "generalist" residential projects implement these principles, such as Globe [031], Biplan [055] or Zénobe Gramme [128], or as found in collective housing projects, such as L'Espoir [060] or Brutopia [097]. Certain projects have the ambition of becoming an eco-neighbourhood, such as Bruyn [100] or Harenberg [136]. Their common objective[2] is to use less resources individually, giving priority to collective services.

[1] See the article devoted to co-housing in be.passive 08, July 2011, p. 32-48.
[2] See be.passive 08, July 2011, p. 40.

Raising of a building on
Rue Vandenbranden [118]:
this project consists of the
passive renovation of the top
floor of a building and the
extension of the roof
(Mr. Vandenbulcke, architect).

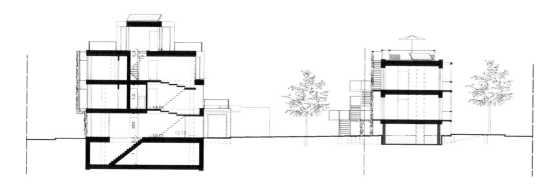

[BATEX 055 – RUE DU BIPLAN] [1]

Rue du Biplan at 1130 Haren | Bxleco1 sprl | Bxleco1 sprl, FHW architectes | Bxleco1, Ecorce

MANAGED CO-HOUSING AND PARTICIPATIVE POOLING

The Rue du Biplan project is a very particular development planned by Claude Rener, Jean-Paul Hermant and Philippe Lauwers, the BxlECO partners. With all their experience in eco-construction, they are working on tomorrow's sustainable living forms and co-housing. But they wanted a more ambitious project, a project going beyond the mere addition of individual, or even grouped needs. They wanted something that would inspire a whole new living experience!

SUSTAINABLE PROJECT SEEKS FAMILIES

Taking a middle path, they came up with a project somewhere between a standard residential development and co-housing. Six families had to be found for the project. The objective of the "grouped habitat" was both to save money and benefit the environment and social contacts. Under the motto "living together is better than living alone", this involved a communal living charter giving priority to occupants behaving in a responsible manner.

A form of exemplarity sought by Coralie, a new occupant, vis-à-vis not just the other co-owners, but also throughout the neighbourhood: "Rather than having a somewhat strange building suddenly inserted into the neighbourhood, we would like to make it a show-window open to the outside and to the immediate vicinity in particular – i.e. complementing our internal momentum with a momentum encompassing our immediate surroundings, our neighbours. This is an integral part of the value-sharing we intend to develop, both on our part vis-à-vis other projects and vice-versa.

SERVICES INCLUDED

Facing south-west, the wooden framed Biplan building is insulated with cellulose in line with the passive standard. The "see-through" apartments offer splendid views, overlooking a small park. The developers have implemented part of the finishings in agreement with the new owners (the apartments were sold as "casco"). Heating is provided by a heat pump in the loft and solar panels, and is distributed via low-temperature underfloor heating. The roofs are planted, providing a communal vegetable garden for herbs and medicinal plants. The 6 families also share a laundry room with a washing machine using solar-heated water, a guest bedroom, a meeting room in the garden, a communal cellar for storing vegetables or growing chicory...

There are also plans for part of the purchase price to be set aside for installing PV panels at a later date – the developers designing the building also thought a bit about the future...

[1] Read the report in *be.passive* 08, July 2011, p. 32 ff.

RE-IMAGINING URBAN LIFE
RUE DU BIPLAN [055]

Claude Rener,
promoter

They have elected to live together in this little-known neighbourhood in the north of Brussels. Together, but in separate apartments. By sharing certain spaces, but also a certain conception of life together. They do not yet know exactly how, but this common building is their starting point...

"We are giving ourselves time to think about how we are going to live collectively, in line with shared values and expectations, step by step..."

Claude Rener, project owner and entrepreneur, is a purist. He has designed this building as a framework. A co-housing framework. "We are looking for a less individualistic, more participative way of living in the city; this should not only generate economies of scale, but also lead to solidarity between inhabitants of all ages and origins." And he knows what he is talking about – for years this is what he has been doing, most of the time sharing an apartment with others. "We initially worked in a sort of utopia, dreaming up an ideal vision of city life, including a few not so normal options, reconsidering for example relationships to land and collective amenities. After working on this for a year, we came up with this project. We gained the support of the authorities who had been following our discussions over the years."

Everything here is thus a little bit idealistic: a bioclimatic architecture, eco-construction, eco-consumption, energy performance (passive standard), rainwater recovery, collective spaces, the location in a little-known neighbourhood (though full of potential and within easy reach), mobility, etc. All that remained was to demonstrate that the options selected were on track from a financial point of view. "This quality needed to be available to everyone, and this project, which is nothing but a milestone between the past, the present and the future, needed to be repeatable elsewhere."

The building has clearly been designed in this spirit, combining private spaces, communal spaces (a garden, a guest room looking out onto the surrounding neighbourhood and opening out onto a vegetable garden on the roof, ...) or purely practical (a cellar, laundry, a separate room currently used as a bicycle garage, but possibly for later use as a children's playroom or a meeting place...).

There's nothing revolutionary about the technology or the materials used. All we wanted to do was to give precedence to simple and ecological solutions, for instance via bulk purchases.

The building is now completed, and all that now needs to be done is to find prospective buyers ready to move in. In the way they want to do it. Coralie: "What we have bought are a few square metres for living privately and a few square metres for living and sharing. What interested us most was the combination, a shared quality of life. If it hadn't been for that, we would not have bought..." And now patiently making contact with this new reality, through joint purchases, individualised finishes and regular meetings which help blend points of views and allow experiences to be swapped. "We are giving ourselves time to think about how we are going to live collectively, in line with shared values and expectations, step by step..."

It's up to them to come up with ideas on how to reconcile the idea of being alone – the nest – with that of being with others – the municipality. It's all about finding the right harmony between privacy and participation. An adventure we are just beginning...

Gaucheret nursery, Rue Rogier [004]: the Gaucheret nursery installs a simple rectangular excavated volume of several patios that extend and multiply an otherwise cramped outside universe (MDW architectes).

06/ CRITICAL MASS

By injecting public funds into different forms of public-private partnerships, Batex is contributing to establishing a critical mass of projects and spreading the word about sustainable construction to a large number of stakeholders.

By word of mouth, from public agencies to private offices, from the drawing board to the building site, Batex has popularised principles of sustainable design and energy-saving targets previously deemed unattainable. Unknown in 2007, the passive standard is now being adopted by more than 7% of new housing projects in Brussels and the floor space of exemplary passive buildings in Brussels is expected to reach more than 150 000 m² by 2014. The passive share there has risen from 21% to 79% over the years. More and more architects and project owners are now coming forward and submitting their Batex applications. On this basis, the Batex projects are showing that it is economically viable to come up with a sustainable architecture benefiting both occupants and the environment.

TRENDS 2007-2011:
PASSIVE STANDARD – NUMBER OF PROJECTS AND AREA IN %

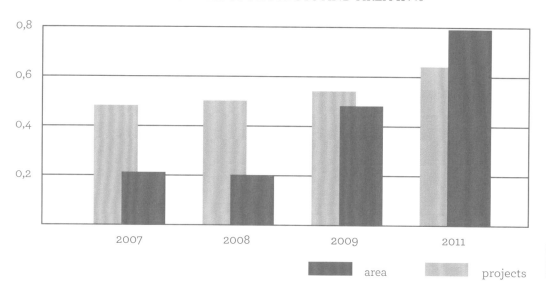

area   projects

"With hindsight, we are realising that this could only have been done here in Belgium. Here the sector provides all the conditions necessary for getting there: our companies – whatever is said about them – have a very high standard; our architects as well. The financial incentives are really attractive. Training is becoming increasingly available at all levels. The public authorities have assumed responsibility. I can see this when I take part in conferences outside Belgium, where we are mainly asked to provide details of this revolutio..."
Sebastian Moreno-Vacca

4 ROUNDS
OF BATEX PROJECTS

156 projects selected,
92 of which involve new buildings and 64 of which are refurbishment or extension projects
371 924 m² of sustainable construction, 66% of which are new and 34% refurbished; and of which 63% come from the private sector (private individuals, non-profit organisations and commercial companies) and 37% from the public sector
44 buildings have been completed,
44 are under construction,
56 are in the design phase or have been abandoned[1].
43 projects involve private houses, with a total floor-space of 9 465 m² and 57 housing units
48 projects involve apartment blocks, with a total floor space of 101 661 m² and 926 housing units
31 projects involve offices, with a total floor space of 112 720 m²
8 projects involve shops, with a total floor space of 16 727 m²
10 projects involve industrial operations, with a total floor space of 19 372 m²
16 projects involve crèches, with a total floor space of 11 859 m²
10 projects involve schools, with a total floor space of 20 388 m²
10 projects come from the healthcare sector, with a total floor space of 49 311 m²
8 projects have a cultural background (including a mosque), with a total floor space of 7 296 m²
There are **3** HORECA projects, with a total floor space of 13 081 m²
1 sports centre and one indoor swimming pool, with a total floor space of 10 044 m²

07/ BRUSSELS
A SUSTAINABLE CITY

The extraordinary variety of urban situations is reflected in the variety of the selected projects, from individual apartments to houses and apartment blocks, from offices to schools, via crèches, sports centres, a mosque, hospitals, etc.

For architect Sebastian Moreno-Vacca, "We are probably witnessing one of the major turning points in the history of the 21st century in the field of energy or sustainable construction. There is nothing like it anywhere else in Europe. This revolution here in Brussels is also the subject of the European PassReg project[2]."

Batex is obviously a voluntary and experimental project. In this respect, it has produced its share of disappointments and stress. But it would be foolish to just sit back and wait. The public authorities are well aware of who, through other regional activities, is participating in the joint effort. This includes the creation each year of some 120 passive houses and apartments and 8 public amenities in the context of the sustainable "Neighbourhood Contracts"[3], the housing and local amenity projects carried out by the SDRB[4] (54 000 and 26 500 m² respectively of passive housing and offices), the construction of 231 000 m² of passive, low or ultra-low-energy housing carried out by the SLRB[5], etc. Batex obviously plays a role here as a multiplie, and practices are changing fast, both in the public and in the private sector.

All of this is in preparation for the transition to the passive energy performance requirement for all new buildings, adopted by the Brussels Government for 2015 (and adopted in advance by the SLRB and SDRB in 2010). And taking up a front-runner position, together with Vorarlberg or Tirol in Austria, Hannover in Germany, in providing architecture of high environmental value.

[1] Figures date from 30 March 2012. The reasons for the abandoned projects have nothing to do with Batex.
[2] European IEE (Intelligent Energy Europe) project: Passive House Regions with Renewable Energies (PASSREG), 2012-2015, http://eaci-projects.eu
[3] www.quartiers.irisnet.be/fr/contrats-de-quartiers-durables
[4] Société de Développement pour la Région de Bruxelles-Capitale, www.sdrb.be
[5] Société du Logement de la Région de Bruxelles-Capitale, www.slrb.irisnet.be

Passive homes in Harenberg [136]: several projects have already responded to the zero energy goal. This is also the ambition for 5 of the 30 housing units at Harenberg (A2M architectes).

Passive social housing on Rue Loossens [016]: the access to the dwellings is from the outside, via the side passage provided by the terrain. Everyone has direct access to their home, with no stair-well to heat (A2M architectes).

ECOLOGY IN DENSELY POPULATED AREAS
TOMORROW'S HOUSING

The first four rounds of Batex have seen grants being given to 91 housing projects, covering nearly a thousand homes and with a total floor space of more than 110 000 m². Housing accounts for more than half of the selected projects, though for only a third of work underway. This is because housing involves a whole range of projects, from small to very large!

BATEX HOMES
IN FIGURES

More than 110 000 m^2 of housing currently being built or planned over 4 years

983 homes, 683 of which are new and 300 refurbished

9% of the annual production of new homes

5.5% of the annual production of refurbished homes

520 passive homes (including 20 zero-energy ones), i.e. 7% of all new homes in Brussels

607 social housing units, 372 of which are passive and 7 zero-energy

376 private homes, 148 of which are passive

3 out of every 4 new Batex homes are passive

From 106 m^2 for the construction of a new passive home Rue Vandenbranden [118] on the roof of an existing building, to more than 13 000 m^2 for the construction of 51 passive apartments and a school in the Rue Simons [137] in Brussels, or 18 000 m^2 as in the case of the refurbishment of the 183 Florair social apartments [061] in Jette.

The demographic upswing[1] in the Brussels-Capital Region will see demand for housing continuing to rise, despite a 9% increase over the last 20 years. The required construction of new homes represents a tremendous opportunity and a duty: Brussels cannot miss this chance of building a sustainable city using the best practices available. Although demand for affordable homes is high and although public housing only accounts for 9% of all homes in Brussels, the public sector participated at a very high level in the call for Batex projects, coming up with

62% of the exemplary homes, at low rents and charges. 94% of these homes are to be found in 48 blocks of apartments. 70% of operations involve new buildings[2].

The average size of the public and private apartments and houses is 113 m^2, i.e. 6% more than the average for new homes in Brussels. This means that the construction of homes offering high energy efficiency and a low environmental footprint does not lead to any trimming of space available to occupants.

[1] Demographic forecasts for Brussels in the period 2010-2020, *Les Cahiers de l'IBSA*, Ministère de la Région de Bruxelles-Capitale, May 2010.
[2] For various reasons, 3 projects are currently on hold, including the large Albatross project [026].

Passive homes on Rue de Suède [034]: thanks to the Batex subsidy, the 30 passive homes (I, 2 and 3 bedroom) of the Midi-Suède project were sold by the BRDA as middle income housing at no additional cost (Urban Platform).

Renovation of the Mommaerts workshops in the Rue Compte de Flandre [022]: this low energy renovation has helped revitalize the neighbourhood; wood fibre insulation has been installed on the rear façade and the building is heated by a pellet boiler (CERAU architectes).

Public housing, Savonnerie Heymans [042]: some innovative features of the project, such as bioclimatic loggias, have been specially designed and extensively tested to meet all the constraints of use (MDW architectes).

01/ LIVING
IN AN APARTMENT BLOCK

An apartment block is the urban object par excellence,
a map of the discontinuities between all-public and all-private.

It is a place for sharing and pooling resources, with its whole ecology based on the principle of "living together", in which agreements and values are constantly being renegotiated. A new factor now appearing are the ecological values.

For the project of converting the former soap factory Savonnerie Heymans [042] into apartments, "the CPAS was very open to our arguments, including energy performance and communal areas, without just pointing to the costs", explained architect Gilles Debrun. "It understood that the wish to give priority to "living together" was of crucial importance in this neighbourhood. It sensed that this project was going to make a great difference and that the extra cost involved would be justified by an improved quality of life and economies of scale in the medium term."

One still comes up against a lot of prejudices against ecological and passive architecture. The variety of situations encountered by Batex makes it possible to make certain adjustments and to verify the "all-round" character of Batex. Available urban space is nowadays often very restricted. You move in, making the most of intermediate open spaces, retreats, sometimes in the form of an outside passageway or terrace, a shared garden, etc. A number of projects are being done in inner courts, where they are creating collective courtyards, gardens or vegetable plots, bicycle parks, ponds, etc. The Batex projects are showing that it is perfectly possible to live well in a densely populated area when there is a link to some form of open space.

Ahmed Bouhnani,
concierge

[TESTIMONY]
DON'T FORGET THE GUIDE!
SAVONNERIE HEYMANS [042]

Commissioned in 2011, the Heymans project and its forty-two apartments blend in nicely with the reality of the neighbourhood. The site, now already well-occupied, is still trying to find its stride - watched over by a "concierge" who does more than just open and close the security doors.
A refurbished building with 4 apartments was selected by Batex in 2007.

"People quickly catch on that the apartments need to be used properly to get the most out of them..."

Just a few years ago, this 60-acre site, near the canal, was an industrial ruin. An old soap factory, which the Heymans family, the owner of the site, made over to the Brussels CPAS in 2006 for housing purposes. To turn it into a coherent project, the CPAS came up with a labyrinth of buildings and open spaces in the inner court, drawing on the creativity of an architectural competition. "In 2005", explained Gilles Debrun, the architect of the selected project, "Al Gore's film was not yet around. Our approach with its clear-cut orientation towards the new demands of sustainable development seduced the selection panel. We presented an ultra-low-energy concept, with co-generation district heating, dual-flow ventilation, thermal solar panels, certain innovations in insulation and the use of solar power and, more importantly, a very diverse living environment, mixing different types of homes with communal areas – a toy park, community garden, playground, vegetable garden, etc. – to create a true habitat nestled in the middle of the neighbourhood."

The result is well worth looking at: a small village consisting of six buildings – four of them new, two refurbished – separated by alleys and small squares, nestled in the heart of the neighbourhood and which visitors discover with certain amazement, passing through the security entrance in the facade of the refurbished building. A resolutely modern complex refreshingly featuring the factory's old chimney, now used for providing ventilation to the underground car park.

The everyday life of its inhabitants is obviously still seeking to find its rhythm in this unusual setting. Tenants for instance still have not gotten used to those strange glass accordion-shaped loggias, which, on the patios of the south-facing facade, are supposed to provide solar heat to the apartments in the winter – provided that they are used the right way, as is the case with any heating or ventilation system. A small manual (in comic book form) handed out to everybody is there to provide initial instructions.

But the secret weapon of the designers is this man who spends the whole day moving around the building and greeting everyone he meets – the concierge. Perhaps it is better to refer to him as a guide, as you will find him talking to you about the technical installations, how they work and how they need to be handled.

With residents and visitors rubbing shoulders every day, he also often needs to remind them about the proper use of the public spaces. And to pass on to the complex's managers and designers the vagaries of the new facilities that can at times be a bit temperamental. "It's not my job to act as the police. My job is to help people to live here, making the most of the various benefits offered and of all the comfort at their disposal. People quickly catch on that the apartments need to be used properly to get the most out of them..."

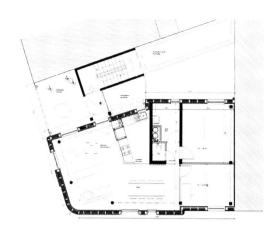

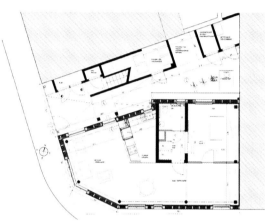

[BATEX 090 – RUE DU LIBRE EXAMEN][1]

Rue du Libre Examen at 1070 Anderlecht | Commune d'Anderlecht | Délices Architectes

A BIT MORE SPACE THAN ORIGINALLY PLANNED

In response to the needs identified in the context of the Aumale-Wayez Neighbourhood Contract in Anderlecht, the Délices architects saw themselves with the responsibility of building passive social housing on two building corner plots left over after the Metro had been built. Commissioned in 2012, Libre-Examen offers a new benchmark for an area undergoing urban renewal.

BUT THERE'S A BIT MORE TO IT...

The original commission was for 4 apartments, but the plot was slightly larger than the budget. Architects and project owners were wise enough not to keep to the plans and to make the most of that "little bit more". They also stress the financial choices made. The budget responds to tenants' priority needs: a single layer of white paint on the walls, basic facilities, but a generous living area, low energy consumption, good views and lots of light.

The clear tongue-in-cheek way the building literally "turns" the corner is coupled with solid constructive logic, meeting the thermal requirements of the passive standard and those of contemporary social housing.

Its architecture provides a mirror between the public area – the entrance, which leads to a sort of urban courtyard (for pushchairs, bicycles, meters, bins, etc.) and the outside staircase – and the private area –, where the apartments face south and are well wrapped up in a wood-lined jacket. Between the two, we find patios facing south-west, so big that residents can sit down there for family meals.

From a construction perspective, the building offers a lesson in passive architecture. Inside, resting on piles, the load-bearing structure of reinforced concrete stays away from insulating caissons made of wood and cellulose enveloping it. The space between the columns and the outer walls creates imaginary partitions making the whole look larger. On the outside, a separate structure supports the patios, avoiding a thermal bridge with the main structure. The architects somewhat regretted having to meet fire requirements which meant that the wooden cladding had to be chemically fireproofed.

TRANSITIONS

The project offers apartments accessible to all from the ground floor. One of its main features is that it manages to integrate multiple transitions between "private" spaces, allowing social interaction. The "being-at-home-feeling" is not brutally shut in by walls – there are windows opening out onto the street or the patio; you can hear the neighbours coming down the stairs (when you are outside); from each floor you can look down into the courtyard, etc.

So many different links between "home" and the outside world, reassuring residents about their status and helping them participate in the life of the building and the street. This forgotten corner is now watched over by a building where the simple luxury of a little more space than "usual" makes you want to live there.

[1] See the Mister Emma report (www.archiurbain.be/?p=377 in *be.passive* 11, July 2012.

Social housing on Avenue Dubrucq [018]: the project has used the public area to sink its Canadian well (B architecten).

Social housing on Rue de la Brasserie [063]: setbacks, folds, terraces, duplication; all new motifs that enable the urban "façade" to fully play its role of both bioclimatic and social transition (R²D² architectes).

02/ UNIQUE URBAN SITUATIONS

Batex projects are all rooted in the city as it exists – densely populated, a multicultural and complex society. Sometimes it's just a case of making the most of very difficult circumstances – small buildings difficult to insulate, facades not getting any sun, buildings in the middle of an inner court, on an embankment, a corner, a slope...

The building density means that residential functions coexist with public amenities, shops, (nursery) schools or offices. This mixed use brings urban services closer together, making them more accessible, just as it makes public transport more efficient.

A loft extension or adding a floor represent refurbishment favourites, as seen in the Nest [050], Rue Vandenbranden [118] or the Rue de la Loi [068] projects. They enable an old building to be upgraded by working on a sensitive surface – the roof – which can be insulated and planted.

Other facades are planted, such as in the Rue Traversière [084] or the Arts & Métiers school [154]. The thickness of the insulated facade also gives architecture a new space for action – retreats, folds, patios, duplication, lots of new designs allowing the urban "facade" to play a full role as a transition between private space and life in the street, as seen in the Brasserie [063], Courses [089], Neerstalle [096] or Moreau [134] projects.

We also find new textures such as at Plume [035], folds and ripples as at Midi-Suède [034] or Cygnes-Digue [039], or the cladding – in wood at Dubrucq [018] or in Cor-Ten steel in the Avenue Moreau [134]. But we also find just simple plaster... and bricks. Other details of such apartment blocks apply to entrance halls, access to cars and garages, spaces reserved for bicycles, the location of the letter boxes (if possible outside the heated building), etc.

Building on a corner – the last plots of land often forgotten in conventional developments – is often a delicate matter in terms of space distribution and compactness. But it also provides the opportunity to vary views and make the most of sunlight. Certain Batex buildings rearticulate the presence of nature – a public good par excellence – on the plot: private and/or communal gardens, green roofs, insect cornices, integrated birds' nests, etc.

Passive public housing on Avenue Rodenbach [007]: these units use the slope of the site to provide a very airy and well-lit parking space below the building. The south-east orientation provides plenty of sunlight to the rear façade. All access is directly from the outside (3A architectes).

Passive social housing on Rue Georges Moreau [134]: this project is based on the urban planning constraints of building sizes, bending the Cor-Ten steel façade (Bogdan & Van Broek Architectes).

ENERGY CONSUMPTION

Heating remains the highest energy consumer, accounting for 69% of the Brussels energy balance (other than transport) and costing more than EUR 587 million a year[1].

Electricity remains the most expensive form of energy – electricity accounts for 31% of the Brussels energy balance (other than transport) and costs more than EUR 800 million a year.

03/ (ENERGY) SAVINGS

85% of the energy consumption of the existing building stock in Brussels goes on heating and hot water.

The compactness of buildings, with terraced housing and apartment blocks predominating, enables the residential sector to have an average net energy demand for heating of 150 kWh/m² a year.

Collective housing allows economies of scale: better prices for building materials, better controlled implementation, prefabrication, centralised heating systems (or even district heating), better monitoring and effectiveness of technical installations, etc.

Batex collective housing projects include 18 zero-energy homes, 487 passive ones, 262 ultra-low-energy ones and 172 low-energy ones. On average, the new projects currently being built have a net heating requirement of 14.5 kWh/m² a year; the corresponding figure for refurbishment projects is 23.4 kWh/m² a year (compared with 150 for the existing building stock).

Batex collective housing projects will be saving some 1 000 000 l of oil a year. Looking only at savings in heating costs, the current rise in energy costs and heating oil prices of 0.90€/l, the Batex grants correspond to at least 6 years of operation.

NET HEATING REQUIREMENT 2007-2011
RENOVATION OF COLLECTIVE HOUSING

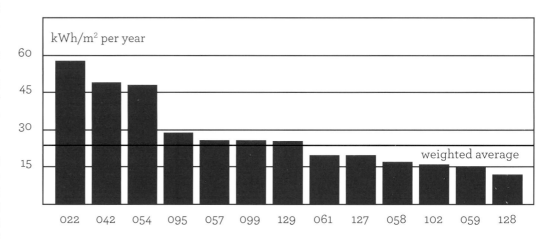

NET HEATING REQUIREMENT 2007-2011
CONSTRUCTION OF COLLECTIVE HOUSING

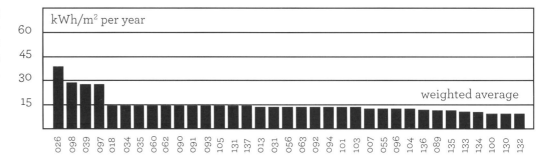

[1] 2009 Brussels energy balance of Brussels Environment.

Passive public housing on Rue de Liège [105]: the staircase is placed outside. The device gives a public character to the landing. It is also an important source of savings because the volume is not heated or insulated and is not subject to the same fire resistance requirements as an indoor stairwell (R²D² architectes).

COLLECTIVE HOUSING AND ENERGY REQUIREMENTS

Net energy requirement for new buildings, heating, average: 14.5 kWh/m² a year

Net energy requirement for refurbished buildings, heating, average: 23.4 kWh/m² a year

PASSIVE CRITERIA FOR RESIDENTIAL BUILDINGS

1/ Energy requirements for heating: the energy requirement for heating must be lower than or equal to 15 kWh/m² a year, equivalent to 1.5 litres of heating oil.

2/ Airtightness: the result of the n50 test must be lower than or equal to 0.6 vol/h (rate of air renewal measured at a difference of 50 Pascal between inside and outside).

3/ Overheating percentage: the overheating percentage in the building (temperature higher than 25°C) must be lower than or equal to 5%.

4/ Primary energy: the building's primary energy – calculated for heating, hot water and any auxiliary heating – must be lower than or equal to 45 kWh/m² a year.

More information on www.maisonpassive.be

L'Espoir passive housing [060]: 100% of collective accomodation uses double flow ventilation (D. Carnoy architect).

Passive public housing in Chaussée de Neerstalle [096]: the units use the bank to create nested duplexes, each with either a garden or a private terrace (B612 architectes).

Passive building on Avenue des Courses [089]: the south façade is extensively glazed. The windows are recessed and in more than 50% of cases are fitted with an external sun protection enabling residents to adjust the brightness and avoid summer overheating while creating a play of light (MDW architectes).

COLLECTIVE HOUSING AND SUSTAINABLE CONSTRUCTION

100 % have additional insulation
100 % use dual-flow ventilation
96 % use solar thermal and / or PV panels
96 % have an on-site cistern or rainwater management system
93 % have designed the building in such a way that it is easy to use a bicycle
84 % have installed some form of protection from the sun or a passive cooling system
82 % use mainly eco building materials
78 % have planted whole or part of the roof

04/ VENTILATION

Practically all selected projects use mechanical dual-flow ventilation. "For us, air quality is one of the qualities taken into least consideration in passive homes", commented Gérard Bedoret, an architect himself living in a passive house [021].

"It has a considerable influence on the quality of life. We just could not do without this carefully considered ventilation made possible by dual-flow ventilation." The BBRI[1] has launched a measuring campaign, the initial results of which show that the quality of pulsed air in mechanical ventilation systems is generally better than outside[2]. Greater attention should however be paid to the choice and maintenance of the filters[3].

In collective housing, the system can be either centralised or decentralised[4]. A central system is more economical – whenever possible placed on the roof away from any source of pollution. Each apartment can be individually regulated, allowing each tenant to manage his own airflow and temperature. A variant of this system allows the air to be distributed in a centralized manner via the installation of heat exchangers and individual post-heating batteries in each apartment, though this is a more complex and expensive system.

It is very important to protect the ventilation ducts during building work. If their ends are not kept closed, dust can accumulate, meaning that they will have to be thoroughly cleaned before the new occupants move in.

To reduce the impact of refurbishment work, the Florair project [061] foresaw a mix of two systems: simple mechanical air extraction for half of the apartments and dual-flow ventilation for the other half.

CONTROLLED MECHANICAL VENTILATION, BUT BY WHOM?

The choice of equipment and the positioning of the ducts should result in the complete avoidance of any transmission of noise or smells. Each occupant must be able to easily and directly regulate his own comfort – i.e. adjusting the airflow and temperature to suit his own needs. In the Rue Fin project [060], a decentralised system was chosen, with each occupant having his own heat exchanger and regulation system.

The ventilation ducts in direct contact with the outside – for the intake and outflow of air – must be well insulated and as short as possible. For engineer Denis Lefébure, "Avoiding ducts or chutes conducting cold air into a heated building needs to remain a basic design principle."[5].

[1] Belgian Building Research Institute.
[2] Samuel Caillou, Paul Van Den Bossche, *Ventilation systems : monitoring of performances on site*, Actes du Passive House Symposium 2011, p. 206. See also *be.passive* 11, June 2012 and the CSS00 info-sheet on eco-construction CSS00: Problématique et enjeux des conforts et de la santé.
[3] See *be.passive* 10, January 2012, p. 78
[4] Denis Lefébure, "Ventilation centralisée ou non ?", in *be.passive* 05, September 2010, p. 74.
[5] See *be.passive* 05, September 2010, p. 76.

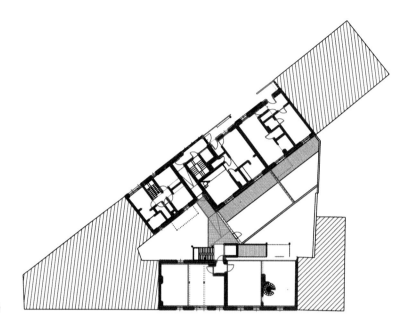

[BATEX 031 – GLOBE] [1]

Chaussée d'Alsemberg 774-776 at 1180 Uccle | Green Immo sprl | FHW architectes | Ecorce

LIKE A COMPASS POINTING SOUTH

The head of the Green Immo property company [2], Esther Jakober, handed over the Globe building in 2011, the first passive and zero-energy development in Brussels.

The building has 13 apartments and office space. Situated in Uccle, the property acts as a bridge between the Rue Bernaerts, onto which 10 of the apartments look, and the Chaussée d'Alsemberg. It revamps a long neglected site, up to now used for parking. Located almost at the tip of a block of housing, it opens like a compass to the south, providing proximity without getting too close.

ECOLOGICAL BUILDING MATERIALS

Built with sand-lime bricks – a building material with a low environmental footprint – the building meets the passive standard. This was the starting point for a larger vision: "We tried to go beyond the purely energy-related aspects, paying attention to all aspects of the building, with a special focus on the choice of building materials. Each one was checked

with regard to its 'grey energy', its impact on the environment, its comfort for occupants, its implementation and its cost", explained Esther Jakober, who already started applying the principles adopted by Batex in 2011 four years earlier, in 2007.

ZERO ENERGY

Technical facilities are foreseen for meeting needs for heating, hot water and cooling, with a cogeneration unit running on rapeseed oil and thermal solar panels used to supply renewable energy. The remainder of the electrical consumption, mainly for pumps and ventilators, is supplied by photovoltaic panels

A CERTAIN AMOUNT OF POOLING AND FLEXIBILITY

The choice of location is not trivial: a building is all the more sustainable when it is located in

an area well-served by public amenities, public transport and local shops. The project replicates this form of pooling by offering owners a laundry with washing machines and dryers, together with a communal space and garden. The apartments are large, with numerous different layouts made possible. A green facade with climbing plants provides a welcome green element on the outside.

[1] See Mister Emma's report, www.archiurbain.be/?p=1136 and the interview with Esther Jakober, "Green Immo", in be.passive 04, June 2010, p. 21.
[2] www.greenimmo.be/globe_techniques.html

[TESTIMONY]

GOOD NEIGHBOURS
AVENUE ZÉNOBE GRAMME [128]

This property developer has discovered a very simple way of attracting loyal and respectful tenants to his apartments, doing everything to make them feel at home... and to get on well with each other. This sometimes requires a bit of imagination and empathy

"We need to help the building trades to evolve. The person I most fear is the old mason who says 'I've always done it like that and it's never been a problem.' It's no good answering 'You're wrong'. But rather: 'we've just discovered that with this particular flick of the wrist it will be even better. And this flick of the wrist, only you, with the experience you have, can do perfectly. We need you.' Who would not be delighted to hear that?"

Yvan Zopp likes being called a property "developer", as it is his intention to develop collective housing concepts which go further than just providing living space at tightly calculated prices. His rates are even a bit higher than those of his competitors. But in his latest housing projects, energy costs are practically nothing as the buildings are ultra-low-energy or even passive, and capture rainwater for resident's use: "When one can say to a potential tenant that the rent is somewhat higher than elsewhere, but that energy costs for heating and hot water hardly cost anything at all – that's quite a calming thought when looked at over a longer period!"

Fascinated by sustainable development for almost ten years now, he is permanently on the look-out for ways of integrating it in his apartment buildings (he already has a portfolio consisting of a dozen buildings, with two more currently under development). His latest "hobby" involves getting neighbours to come together more, for example by systematically providing communal areas for tenants – laundries, sports rooms, reading corners, places for getting together, a bicycle room, etc. But also via a blog specifically for an apartment building, where tenants can pass on messages, or – as in SEL (local exchange systems) schemes – giving neighbours the opportunity of posting their small ads, like asking for assistance or offering low-key services like babysitting, watering plants when people are away or car-pooling.

"Our primary commercial objective is to have tenants stay as long as possible in the apartments. And they stay when they find what they expect – the right level of comfort, a feeling of being at home, and readily available solutions in the case of any problem.

The quintessence of all these ideas is to be found in the ongoing refurbishment of an old industrial building that has just been nominated as a "2011 exemplary building". Seventeen apartments and 450 m2 of office space offering top energy performance (either low-energy or passive) and designed to foster residents coming together.

"We very often find that when a tenant reports a problem to us, it would have been much easier for him to have simply knocked on his neighbour's door. In many cases the neighbour would be willing and able to help him – and much quicker than we could do it. The communal laundry room and sports room have just this objective – facilitating contacts. And on top of this there are always other aspects such as saving money or doing something for one's health. And of course such communal areas must not be rooms that are difficult to get to or uninviting. Provide them with natural light, decorate them nicely – and people will start feeling just as much at home there as in their own apartments."

He is currently testing a combined laundry – sports room, thereby increasing the opportunities for people to get together.

But his thoughts and ideas go even further: "More and more people, even from the middle classes, are finding it difficult to find comfortable accommodation in Brussels. One possible answer in our view is flat-sharing. We are thinking along the lines of offering apartments designed in this spirit. Three or four similar-sized rooms, giving each tenant the same amount of space, and with an interior layout fostering harmonious sharing between people who don't even know each other at the start. We are thinking for example of older people wanting to live at home and who would be willing to share with a family. Hybrid schemes inspired by such initiatives as Abbeyfield or 'grouped habitat'".

This also has the chance of becoming exemplary.

Renovation on Avenue Besme [054]: the project involves the renovation of a remarkable former art déco mansion into housing and offices. The architects have succeeded in reconciling the imperatives of architectural heritage conservation.
(A-cube architecture).

Renovation and heightening of a building on Rue de la Loi [068]: the building has been heightened with three levels of new passive homes that significantly improve the insulation of the roofs and provide a mix that is all too absent in this business district (Synergy international).

05/ FROM LARGE PROJECTS TO MINI-PROJECTS

The average size[1] of public housing projects has increased from 10 units in 2007 to 17.6 in 2011, whereas the corresponding figure for the private housing sector has remained about 8 units.

Batex is gradually moving away from large projects whose implementation or possible cessation – a common hazard in the industry – would significantly impact the overall balance.

The construction experience gained over the last four years shows that technical and financial aspects are easier to deal with than expected – it's just a question of learning. By contrast, bringing co-owners together to jointly submit a Batex application seems to be a lot more difficult – apart from the co-housing projects, there are for instance no exemplary refurbishment projects involving condominium blocks. This is however an enormous market sector.

[1] Excluding Albatros [026] and Florair [061].

Renovation of a listed building on Avenue Ducpétiaux [077]: with a listed façade by architect Hankar, the renovation of this house was directed mainly at reorienting the house in relation to its garden. The energy challenge of the project was to reach the low energy standard without touching the street façade or the original interior mouldings (S. Closson, architect).

PART OF THE URBAN LANDSCAPE

EXEMPLARY HOUSES

[CHAPTER 04]

Once upon a time it was the smallest unit of a city. Today a house is an almost unaffordable way of life: opportunities are too rare and too expensive, building sites hard to organize and construction complex. After the office sector, however, it is individual housing projects that are completed the fastest. With 9 465 m² distributed over 57 units, individual housing accounts for 6% of all Batex housing. 90% of investment in this area is by individuals, mainly in the renovation of houses dating from the early twentieth century and which need to be isolated or extended.

House renovation on Rue Docteur Leemans [048]: this fifties house with its bel étage first floor living area has undergone a renovation focused on reducing the energy needed for heating (FHW architects).

Renovation of a listed house on Avenue Ducpétiaux [077]: the front façade is insulated from the inside on 3 of the 4 levels, and new window frames (S. Closson, architect).

Passive house on Rue Verre-winkel [083]: the only Batex 'detached' project, this 168 m² house is located at the top of Uccle Cemetery. To take advantage of the wooded site, the living area is on the first floor (P. Blondel, architect).

House renovation on Rue Traversière [084]: the rigorous approach in terms of green building has permitted a focus on the optimum and maximum use of sustainable, non-toxic and easily recyclable materials (atelier d'architecture Matz-Haucotte).

House renovation on Rue de la Clinique [045]: the "Maisie" project retains the neoclassical character of its façade thanks to interior insulation. With the ground floor extending uninterrupted to the garden, the green space penetrates into the heart of the living rooms. (D. Dardenne, L. Collignon, architects)

The region counts nearly 200 000 buildings, all types combined. They are relatively old, with only 16% of all homes built after the first oil crisis. Brussels' housing stock is the least well insulated of Belgium's three regions (except the roofs) and Belgium itself is the laggard in Europe. Fuel poverty is increasing. With its old and inappropriate buildings and its growing population, Brussels needs to build new homes, but also renovate old ones. 62% of individual dwellings in the Batex scheme are renovations.

The Batex house averages 175 m² for 4 people. Household budgets – often of young couples with families – are strained. For those discovering the world of construction on this occasion, it is no easy path. Finding competent companies remains difficult, especially for small sites, and many people feel outpaced by today's technical innovations. "My job has taken me to visit a lot of houses renovated in this pioneering spirit", says owner Benjamin Clarysse [122]. "This of course reassures me as to the relevance of our project." Batex also provides reassurance, but "and yet I have sometimes a hard time believing that this all makes sense, that we are not unreasonable in believing that such a project holds water, and that it is feasible and realistic in the long term."

Benjamin Clarysse,
promoter and inhabitant

THEY TOOK THE TIME TO CALCULATE EVERYTHING VERY ACCURATELY
RUE MASSAUX [122]

They used to live in a quiet village near Leuven. They chose to move to Brussels, to put an end to commuting and congestion. By calculating as finely as possible they are in the process, after several years of maturing their plan, to start a renovation that should offer their small family a house that is frugal but comfortable for quite some time. A courageous bet on the future... and one to copy.

"Finding competent companies remains difficult when one is not introduced into these circles, and many people feel outpaced by the technical and theoretical concepts evoked there."

They both work in Brussels; he in an environmental NGO, she in public transport. They used to spend a crazy amount of time (and money) in transport between Leuven and the offices and nurseries in the capital. So, off to Brussels.

At first they rented. Then, in 2006, came the idea of buying. They fell in love with a modest house in a poor but very friendly part of Schaerbeek. Acquired cheaply, the house was full of problems, but at least they were in their own home. After a few years, the children came and renovation was needed. They also by now knew their home well enough to see that such a renovation, to be sustainable, would necessarily be a major one.

By saving on transportation (bike, metro, Cambio), they put together the beginning of a budget. But this would not be enough. So they went looking for what premiums were available (boosted by the Coteaux-Josaphat Sustainable Neighbourhood Contract) and willing bankers. They are well placed to know that the energy performance and environmental efforts can ramp up grant amounts. The renovation project took shape little by little on the basis of 'enlightened' advice and certain 'caprices' of the owners (Litte: 'I wanted to keep the old moulding'). Objective: to get the best energy performance possible with a view to the long-term savings and the immediate costs.

The initial estimates were astronomical. Litte: "It soon became clear that we would have to calculate very tightly and make maximum use of all existing premiums and banking conditions. And also find an architect and a contractor to help us control costs...". Not easy to find the right technical partners – architect, contractor, special trades – when they realized that they would have to fight for months on a daily basis for a parking space in this cramped neighbourhood and justify every euro spent. Benjamin: "All the experienced contractors were 30% more expensive. The offers were all between 200 000 and 250 000 euros. We found only one who was really interested in the site as a whole. But for him, like us, a very low energy renovation was a first. Collaborating on an exemplary building was a way of showcasing himself, of earning a nice visiting card."

Anyway, the renovation budget, prepared according to the criteria imposed by the various public grants, would be a good quarter covered by Brussels subsidies. But even then it would still devour a small salary in mortgage repayments. A bold gamble that Litte summarized in six Excel pages, itemizing estimated costs item by item, phasing the work and payment terms and grant payments. The result was a score that left little room for wrong notes: supplements, delays, postponements in incoming payments... Benjamin on his side was realistic: "We'll probably have to postpone certain items – the outdoor terrace, cupboards and some finishing here and there – until later, for lack of money." And he prepared to free up a little time every day to keep a constant eye on the work where, he knew, every detail would be important, both for energy efficiency and for cost control...

House renovation on Rue Rubens [043]: generally it is possible to insulate roofs, as well as rear façades. The Rubens house reaches a net heating need of 36kWh/m²/year, by partially insulating the front façade, which reduces heat loss and will makes it possible, as work progresses, to come close to 30kWh/m²/year (S. Filleul S., A. De Nys).

01/ LIVING IN THE GARDEN, INVITING NATURE BACK INTO TOWN

Today's house, whether newly built or renovated, no longer faces the road, as it once did, but rather its courtyard or garden. That's where it draws its light, that's the side its intimate spaces open out onto, and from where it draws its resources.

It is often on this side that there is more freedom to act, build an extension, insulate from the outside, etc. 100% of the Batex houses have insulated their rear façades from the outside.

Most houses have a town garden, as at Ducpétiaux [077] or an attractive courtyard as at Massaux [122], which is more than enough to reorganize the entire house.

Access to green spaces, as at Verrewinkel [083], is a rare privilege in Brussels. Moreover, it is on the roof that certain of them reconstitute their micro-ecosystems; 40% of individual Batex dwellings have introduced biodiversity measures on their land. Sometimes the physical setting, boxed in or cramped, is demanding and defines the project, as at Rue De Vrière [044], Rue du Fort [106] and Rue Vandernoot [125].

02/ PARTY WALLS REVISED AND CORRECTED

Most Batex projects are part of a larger pre-existing building and need to address issues of heat transfer... including in particular party walls. Until the advent of passive building, these were considered as non-heat losing as they were heated from both sides.

This remains true today, except that passive houses are without conventional heating systems and need to take seriously the risk of the next-door house being unoccupied... and unheated. Hélène Nicodème [081]: "We moved into the building which was completed in March 2011. Just then the outside weather was particularly cold. No luck, during this period the house next door was for sale, empty and practically unheated. We clearly felt this. The day the neighbour's heating was restarted, things went back to normal..." Conclusion: one needs to plan a minimum insulation for party walls, which somewhat reduces the living space, and size the heating on the need to reheat a house after the heating has been off for a time.

Some projects are counting on the subsequent construction of the adjoining plot. Meanwhile, two solutions: either over-insulate (even temporarily) the wall, like Wauters [017], but this makes financial sense only if the situation is set to last, or to accept the house operating in 'low energy' mode before becoming fully passive with the construction of the house next door. This is the choice of architect Gerard Bedoret [021], who further emphasizes the importance of regulation of a passive house: "We have gotten used to over-sized installations of traditional housing, but in passive housing, we stick to a simple post-heating radiator. This requires us to be much more precise and careful with regulation. It is important to find the right measure and to make sure (with a very small margin of safety) that the right supplementary heat will be there very precisely when it is needed..."

Another problem is to avoid (new construction) or decrease (in renovation) thermal bridges in contact with foundations and façades. Case-by-case study is essential.

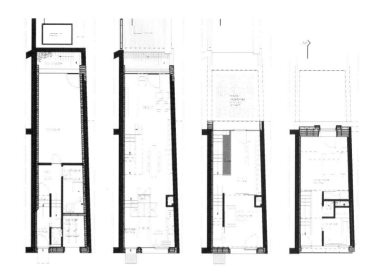

[BATEX 021 – MONTAGNE SAINT-JOB][1]

Montagne de Saint-Job 35 at 1180 Uccle | Bedoret Gérard, Damas Véronique | Gérard Bedoret architecte | Gérard Bedoret

THE PATIENCE
OF THE PARTY WALL

The architect Gérard Bedoret and his partner unearthed a 106 m² plot near the Place Saint Job at Uccle, a neighbourhood known for its picturesque penchant of its particular PPAS[2], which imposes in particular a "French-style" mansard roof...

To the southwest: the first neighbouring house of a fragment of street. To the north, a plot to be built upon soon. Between the two, an average of 4.3 m for the passive house the architect wants to build. Designed for two people (but convertible into "four persons"), the house develops upward along two interconnecting staircases, over 150 m² without any compartmentalization.

SPATIAL FLUIDITY
The volume is fully open and takes full advantage of the qualities of the thermal ambiances of passive construction. Air circulates freely in the house, from a ventilation system connected to a 'Canadian well' underground heat exchanger planted at the bottom of the garden. At the top of the southeast façade, wooden shutters reinterpret the Mansard roof and provide protection against both the sun and nosy passers-by. Otherwise, the elevations are glazed, allowing an abundant east-west light to penetrate deep into the building. The cross-section takes advantage of the terrain and its 4 m slope to provide a sunken courtyard which lights a large basement and to cover the living room with a green roof. Real precision work.

UNTIL THE NEIGHBOUR COMES
The neighbour having postponed his building plans, the house is still not passive. Should one over-insulate? The architect said no, given the narrowness of the plot. In agreement with Brussels Environment, the house originally designed to be passive will indeed classify as Batex, but very low energy (27 kWh/m² per year), until the neighbour erects his building.

MATERIALS
The walls and floors are made entirely of certified wood composite joists. The house is insulated by 30 cm of cellulose. The new party wall is constructed in solid cellular concrete blocks covered with clay on the inside, 6 cm of PUR insulation and whitewashed terracotta blocks on the outside. The existing party wall is lined on the inside to a thickness of 10 cm and closed with a continuous airtight seal. The cladding is in cedar.

A rainwater tank has been installed on the embankments, which also collects the neighbour's roof runoff, which is sufficient for the toilets, a washing machine and for maintenance. A street level room has been made for bikes. This little house has everything a big one has: it is already a must for the "energy walks" organized[3] in the neighbourhood.

Winner in the 'other small dwellings category', the architect is pleased that the experience gained in building his own house has allowed him to work much faster on his new commissions. "A small risk here is that of reproducing solutions that have become familiar while construction approaches are constantly evolving..." And even if the extra work is not necessarily covered by the grant awarded to designers for small projects, "this does not prevent one from playing the game..."

[1] See the details in be.passive 06, January 2011, p. 40.
[2] Urban planning regulations, Plan Particulier d'Affectation des Sols = Specific Land Use Plan.
[3] See the residents' association website, www.acqu.be

[TESTIMONY]
SNUG AND WARM, SIDE BY SIDE
RUE MONTAGNE SAINT-JOB [021]

This house was built on one of the few pieces of land still available in this typical and highly sought-after corner of Uccle. As an architect, he wanted it soft and comfortable like all passive houses. This called for a little more ingenuity than expected...

"For us, air quality is one of the qualities taken into least consideration in passive homes. But it has a considerable influence on the quality of life. In future we just cannot do this carefully considered ventilation made possible by dual-flow ventilation."

Brussels is numb with cold. It is one of those periods when, in families, one feels a particular need to snuggle up close to one other. For homes, it's rather the same; they heat themselves largely by sitting tight together, with the party walls between. A form of conviviality and thermal solidarity, if you like.

In any case, that is what architect Gérard Bedoret had calculated in designing this house with passive ambitions for himself and his wife. Alas, his PHPP* accounts were thrown out of kilter when his neighbour, who at the time was planning to build with a party wall, postponed his project. "This threw out all my calculations. To arrive at 15kWh/m² per year, I could of course add thirty or forty centimetres of insulation on the future party wall, like on a normal façade, but then I would lose that much of an already narrow interior space; and I would lose my investment as soon as my neighbour decided to build..."

Result: the energy performance is for now limited to about 27 kWh/m² and Gérard will wait for his neighbour in order for his house to fully achieve its objectives. But he is not losing sleep over it. It is true that the house has already been certified passive and zero energy, since everything has been implemented in accordance with these standards and that the construction of the neighbouring building is not the responsibility of the designer.

What annoyed him more at the start of his project was the need for additional heat, which would have to be provided. Not just a simple post-heating radiator as in a passive house. The boost would have to be somewhat more generous. But there again, the solution would be temporary. "A small central heating installation and a few radiators would have done the trick. But I wanted a solution that would lend itself better to the future passive performance of the building."

The architect then went looking for ideas via Brussels Environment which, through the Batex coaching, put him in touch with a specialist office which was abreast with the latest discoveries in this field. "They made me a little comparative calculation – with supporting documentation – of the different options, taking into account performance, operating modes, embodied energy, CO_2 emissions etc. In this way I came across this little airtight gas insert, which if necessary can heat the whole house in minutes. It's a bit oversized for the needs of a passive building, but there is also a visual pleasure involved."

A surprising but seductive solution (the equipment is sold mainly as decoration for traditional buildings), which he now offers to his own customers: "Everyone dreams of a traditional fireplace, even in a very low energy or passive building." The moral of this story: that energy performance of buildings is another area where we learn by using our feet.

03/ WHAT NEW MATERIALS?

Batex gives pride of place to the materials included in the publications of the Dutch NIBE[1]. Other reference frameworks exist and are sometimes used by the winners.

Generally, the use of many materials that are still rare in the traditional market is more common in Batex: 97% of projects make significant use of ecological materials. Peter Somers notes that we are witnessing an explosion of green materials: "Everyone realizes now that this is the direction in which we must go. Suddenly, the products are becoming more diverse and affordable."

Here we find: cellulose (insulation blown from shredded paper), FSC and PEFC[2] certified woods, insulation made from wool or wood shavings, wood, hemp or flax, solvent-free paints, radon-free plasters, clay finishings, wood/straw walls or walls in lime/hemp concrete, calcium silicate blocks, etc. Certain architectural choices avoid chemical treatments on the woodwork.

For engineer Denis Lefébure, "suppliers have evolved: they are now offering better performance materials, more complete technical documentation and new products." Not always easy to find? For contractor Alain Demol, "you need to find and work with merchants who have a more proactive approach and who are themselves looking for this kind of product." Contractor Claude Rener goes one further: "We have now accumulated sufficient experience of each of these products, and demand is such that the channels are now well organized. These ancient materials, adapted to today's standards, offer a real alternative to industrial materials often derived from petrochemicals…" Some materials, however, do not yet have technical approval, which is problematic for the reception of buildings by official bodies.

Which is not to say that more traditional materials – think of masonry, concrete, but also mineral or synthetic insulating materials – are not absent from Batex. To objectify their choices, the designers of the Etangs Noirs homes [132] and the MD2E offices [066] used software[3] to analyse the parameters of embodied energy, greenhouse gas emissions and the consumption of water or other natural resources, along with renovation and recycling capacities. These parameters are aggregated in a 'score' reflecting the overall impact of the material. These studies revalorize certain materials deemed non-ecological in the NIBE reference framework. For architect Vincent Szpirer, "one does not need to limit oneself to wood. Other environmentally equivalent but more traditional solutions also exist. It is important, in order to lower the cost of passive construction, to be able to use building companies which have mastered traditional techniques." A discussion to be continued in the context of the exemplary buildings...

Which does not stop one asking: can a building be intuitively recognized as sustainable when, like the dwelling units in the Rue du Pépin [062], they are clad with an attractive but poisonous copper skin? So much virtue otherwise[4] but then parading in a material that it is stolen from railway tracks?

[1] Nederlands Instituut voor Bouwbiologie en Ecologie, see Tools.
[2] Certifications (Forest Stewardship Council and Programme for the Endorsement of Forest Certification schemes) that guarantee the sustainable origin of the wood.
[3] For example www.ecobau.ch, www.eco-bat.ch or http://beacv.be
[4] The choice of copper was made during construction and involved compensatory modifications in order to remain globally sustainable.

Extension of a dwelling on Rue de la Poterie [050]: attic extension or heightening is a favourite form of renovation, as in the Nest project that enlarges the top floor of a building and achieves a very low energy level (N. Stragier, MET architectuur).

House renovation on Rue Rubens [043]: the house is a typical 19th century terraced house. For the occupants, proper insulation and use of bio-ecological materials were obvious. But they also wanted to preserve the character of the house, especially the authentic espagnolette windows of the façade and the ceiling mouldings (S. Filleul S., A. De Nys).

INDIVIDUAL HOUSING AND SUSTAINABLE CONSTRUCTION

100 % have reinforced insulation
98 % use double-flow ventilation
91 % use solar thermal and/or photovoltaic panels
89 % have installed a cistern or manage rainwater on their plots
88 % use mostly eco-materials
78 % have installed sunscreens or passive cooling devices
71 % have adapted their homes to facilitate bike use
51 % have planted all or part of their roof

INDIVIDUAL HOUSING AND
ENERGY REQUIREMENTS

Net heating requirement,
new buildings,
average 16.7 kWh/m² per year

Net heating requirement,
renovations, average 27.2 kWh/m²
per year

Renovation of an apartment house on Rue Gérard [058]: the need to renovate the different apartments, the degraded condition of certain structures and new acoustic norms led the architect to insert new floors. He opted for a semi-prefabricated solution using pre-stressed concrete joists and wood fibre intra-joists (E. Draps, architect).

House renovation on Rue Huberti [051]: "In renovation, each project is unique. Let's use the principles worked out by passive buildings – insulation, ventilation, airtightness – accepting that sometimes the passive standard is not economically or technically reasonable." (Olivier Alexandre, architect).

04/ SAVINGS AND ENERGY

The individual Batex dwelling units consist of 2 zero-energy, 26 passive, 20 very low energy and 9 low energy dwellings. Their average fuel efficiency is impressive, since, in the renovated dwellings, the heating need is reduced to one-fifth and in new construction it is approaching the passive standard.

On average, new homes have a net heating requirement (BEN_{ch}) of 16.7 kWh/m² per year (as against 80 to 100 for new PEB), renovations have a net heating requirement of 27.2 kWh/m² per year (against 150 for existing ones). Overall, the Batex initiative represents for individual dwellings an annual savings of more than 100 000 litres of oil. In considering only the heating savings, the current rise in energy costs and the price of 0.90 €/l, Batex subsidies represent less than 7 years of operation.

NET HEATING REQUIREMENT 2007-2011 RENOVATION OF INDIVIDUAL

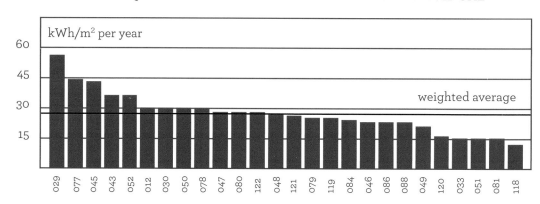

kWh/m² per year

weighted average

029 077 045 043 052 012 030 050 078 047 080 122 048 121 079 119 084 046 086 088 049 120 033 051 081 118

NET HEATING REQUIREMENT 2007-2011 NEW BUILD OF INDIVIDUAL

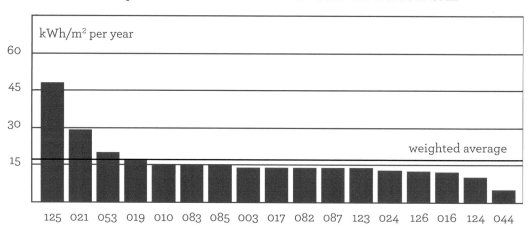

kWh/m² per year

weighted average

125 021 053 019 010 083 085 003 017 082 087 123 024 126 016 124 044

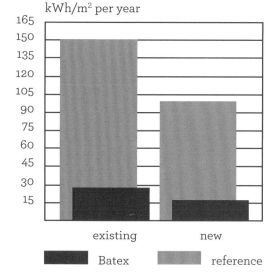

kWh/m² per year

existing   new

■ Batex   ■ reference

Extension of a dwelling on
Rue de la Poterie [050]:
two apartments have been
renovated and expanded with
an additional volume on the
top floor. The green roof and
the consistent opting for
ecological materials clearly
illustrate the attention to
environmental quality
(N. Stragier, MET architectuur).

House renovation in Chaussée de Forest [046]: the architect has redesigned the layout of the building to enlarge the living spaces and open them towards the garden, a logical choice that is all the more sensible in that it expands the house (G. Vilet, architect).

House renovation on Avenue du Diamant [033]: reaching passive standard in renovation means working on eliminating thermal bridges, for example by rebuilding a brand new structure insulated from the inside as here (Modelmo, M. Opdebeek, architect).

House renovation on Rue Crocq [079]: the back façade is insulated from the outside, the front façade from the inside. Solar thermal and photovoltaic panels take advantage of the south-west facing front roof (FHW architectes).

05/ RENOVATION

Who is renovating in Brussels? Of the 500 000 occupied dwellings in Brussels, 75% are apartments, 25% are single-family homes. Brussels consists 58.5% of tenants and 41.5% of owner occupiers[1].

Owner-occupiers are obviously more sensitive than others to the sustainable renovation of their property because they enjoy the greater comfort and energy savings resulting from the renovation process.

Brussels has over 120 000 single family homes that need to be renovated and brought up to present-day standards. This is where Batex renovation is also the most frequent. If projects are numerous, they remain small, however: with

43 projects totalling 9 400 m², individual housing accounts for only 3% of the floor space involved and 4% of the grants. Far from drying up regional funds, these projects contribute to the subtle and complex renovation of Brussels' housing fabric.

[1] Rented housing consists of 90% apartments, 6% houses and 4% kots (student rooms). *Dossier du baromètre conjoncturel n° 21: Observatoire des Loyers. Enquête 2010. Un outil scientifique d'analyse du marché locatif privé en Région de Bruxelles-Capitale* (2011).

[BATEX 046 – THE DRUGSTORE][1]

chaussée de Forest 96 at 1060 Saint-Gilles | Kirschfink Elin, Leurquin Georges | Gwenola Vilet | Escape + M. Montulet

KEEPING ONE'S HEAD DOWN

This little town house right in the middle of Saint-Gilles is representative of thousands of houses needing renovation in Brussels. They offer a charm one wants to retain, are often very well located (here, the neighbourhood has everything you need in terms of shops and public transport), and yet... you have to demolish a lot. The consolation: that this permits very in-depth renovation.

This is what the owners and architect Gwenola Vilet did, without touching the front wall, given that the shop front – an old chemist's – and the façade were listed buildings.

OPENING TO THE GARDEN IF POSSIBLE

When the house has in addition an attractive and well-oriented garden (here: to the south-east), all the mechanics of modern family life then turn their back to the street (and to the untouchable front façade). The architect has redesigned the inside of the building to enlarge the living space and open up the garden, a logical choice that is all the more logical for expanding the house. The ground was excavated to give a new ground floor. Precise insulation of the envelope creates buffer zones between the new rebuilt areas at the back and the area retained at the front. These modifications enable the small terraced house of yesteryear to take full bioclimatic advantage of its urban situation.

EFFECTIVE INSULATION

Technically, the work on the airtightness achieved an impressive result, with n50 tests measuring 0.95 vol/h – where the owner was looking for 2-3 – thanks to a long and painstaking hunt for leaks by the owners, who had no prior experience! The insulation of the roof and the façade, the placing of new window frames at the rear and refurbishment of the old façade windows have reduced the heating need to 21 kWh/m^2 per year.

WHAT ABOUT THE FRONT FAÇADE?

All renovations involving terraced properties have one sensitive area: the insulation of the front façade. Built in 1916, the bluestone-framed shop window is a remarkable element which was not to be touched. The façade was insulated inside and simulation checked the moisture flow to ensure the sustainability of the joists embedded in the existing wall.

The renovation of old façades also keeps certain trades alive. The woodwork of the window was renovated, shifting from simple to double glazing, a change not detectable at first glance. This project is also exemplary in showing that contributing to a living heritage does not mean freezing it in a supposedly 'original' state, but adapting to the demands of modern life by tapping into the knowledge and skills of craftsmen and architects.

[1] Read the report in *be.passive* 07, April 2011, p. 69.

Renovation of a building on Rue Royale Sainte-Marie [099]: the work of preservation of heritage façades has been extended inside, for example using the vocabulary of plaster mouldings to integrate ventilation ducts. Particular attention has been paid to the airtightness of each apartment (P. Abel, architect).

06/ THE LITTLE HERITAGE?

How does one preserve the little heritage of neo-classical or turn-of-the-century houses, the heritage of the thirties or that of the modernist period?

The architecture of those years induced a use of the building which was adapted to the different comfort zones that its construction implied, some walls for example being colder than others. This has become very difficult today, where buildings are often 100% occupied (with attics converted into bedrooms, etc.) and where everyone wants to be warm and comfortable everywhere in the building. Under these conditions, some buildings from the thirties, built to save money, have in fact become very expensive to live in.

Sometimes insulating a building reduces or obscures its original style. While often welcome to the rear, insulation is often a more delicate question on the front of the building. There is a consensus to preserve the details of nineteenth and twentieth century brick façades, but the delicate writing of the fifties could disappear under a coat of insulation if not appreciated at its true value. Rue des Archives [081], owner Hélène Nicodème puts the question: "For the outside, we used insulation material with a coating on top. On reflection, I wonder if you don't lose something of the character of the street and neighbourhood..."

One avenue for approaching the goal of zero carbon in renovation is to adapt the heating installation to renewable energy: heat pump, geothermal, solar, biomass (rapeseed, pellets, wood, etc.). But better to first reduce the energy requirements: a simple transfer of energy dependence from fossil fuels to biomass, for example, does not remove the economic dependency. It also induces additional competition between food, industrial and energy uses, as seen for agrofuels[1] or in timber. Finally, in order to reserve the energy available in the future for renovated buildings, it is important to reduce heating requirements in new construction with the passive house standard.

[1] See Energy Info Sheet ER 13: Biofuels or agrofuels, http://documentation.bruxellesenvironnement.be

House renovation on Rue Docteur Leemans [048]: this deep house opens up onto an attractive west-facing garden. Various measures serve to limit overheating: a vegetation cover on the front façade, while the rear façade has been fitted with external sun protection (FHW architectes).

07/ THE WORK OF RENOVATING THE "ENVELOPE"

The main objective of work on the outer structure or "envelope" of a building is to ensure the continuity of insulation and sealing. When this is possible within urban planning constraints, it is simplest to work from the outside.

This is the path taken for the Rue des Archives renovation [081] and all the back walls of both the homes and the offices of the Ligue des Familles [138], and the social housing at Florair [061] and Rue Strauwen [095]. It has the effect of changing the facing material and gives a new presence to the building.

The ability to fully or partially insulate the outer walls determines the overall energy efficiency of a renovation. This is what is shown by the graph indicating the net heating requirements (BEN$_{ch}$) of housing and office space after renovation.

The Telex offices [006] have lined an existing façade with a second glass skin – hence with little insulating effect, the rest of the building being classified: its BEN$_{ch}$ is 71 kWh/m² per year; the Mommaerts building [022], sandwiched between two others, has not insulated façades and reduces to 58; Mundo-B [067] has minimized costs by opting for regular thickness insulation and reached 54; in Avenue Besme [054] and Ducpétiaux [077], heritage constraints have not permitted the insulation of the front façades. Generally it is possible to insulate roofs, as well as rear façades. The Rubens house [043] reaches a BEN$_{ch}$ of 36 kWh/m²

because it partially insulates the front, which reduces heat loss and can approach, as a function of the work, 30 kWh/m², as in Rue Piks [030] or Rue Traversière [084].

Full insulation, with the reduction of thermal bridges, like at the Ligue des Familles [138], can approach 20 kWh/m², or almost passive, like the offices at Science-Montoyer [107] where the compactness is high. To achieve passive level in

renovation, it is necessary to eliminate thermal bridges, for example by cutting the façade from the floors. This fairly delicate operation was undertaken for the house in Rue Huberti [051] or the offices in Rue Vanpé [014]. Or else one can increase the thickness of the insulation where possible, as in the house in Rue des Archives [081], or by rebuilding a brand new insulating structure on the inside as at Diamant [033], or on the outside as at the school on Chaussée de Merchtem [150] or above the existing building as at Avenue Rousseau [149]. These latter renovations have also installed triple glazing.

NET HEATING REQUIREMENT ACCORDING TO THE TYPE OF INSULATION USED IN REFURBISHMENT

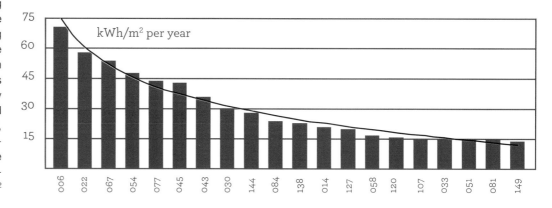

kWh/m² per year

75 — 60 — 45 — 30 — 15

006 022 067 054 077 045 043 030 144 084 138 014 127 058 120 107 033 051 081 149

08/ DOES EFFECTIVE RESTORATION HAVE TO BE PASSIVE?

Public and private resources are limited. We need therefore to be effective to make optimal use of them. The trend over the successive editions of Batex show that the net heating need in renovation is coming close to $25\,\mathrm{kWh/m^2}$ for individual housing and could even go below 20 in collective housing (and $35\,\mathrm{kWh/m^2}$ for amenities buildings and 42 for offices).

This corresponds to reductions in heating consumption of 80% for housing and 60 to 70% for other buildings. Each Batex-renovated m^2 reduces fuel oil consumption by 10.7 litres a year, more than in new construction.

Purists will say that this is not passive. But should we be worried? For Olivier Alexandre [051], "In renovation, each project is unique. Let's use the principles worked out by passive buildings – insulation, ventilation, airtightness – accepting that sometimes the passive standard is not economically or technically reasonable. Let's not be dogmatic, we arrive in any case at excellent performances." Renovation needs are such that it is better to have lots of very low energy renovations than a handful of more difficult passive renovations. The fact is that moving below 25 kWh/m² per year adds sharply to the costs. But the challenge that needs to mobilize resources (public and private) is the massive reduction in energy requirements, especially where they lead to fuel poverty, when some tenants are forced to consume hundreds of kWh/m²... while remaining cold! Batex shows that, without going as far as passive renovation, reducing this consumption by a factor of 5 or 10 is an accessible, useful and reproducible social objective[1]. Let's not be fetishists. Batex does not impose passive level renovation!

[1] In Belgium, several examples of best practices in home renovation have been documented in the federal research project Low Energy Housing Retrofit (LEHR), www.lehr.be

Renovation of a building on Rue Royale Sainte-Marie [099]: the project has renovated the 3 upper levels of a typical Brussels house to produce 3 dwelling units. Using mostly natural materials, expert craftsmanship was needed to incorporate the insulation and ventilation into the existing eclectic architecture. The existing window frames have been maintained and repaired (P. Abel, architect).

RENOVATION OF INDIVIDUAL HOUSING: NET HEATING REQUIREMENT

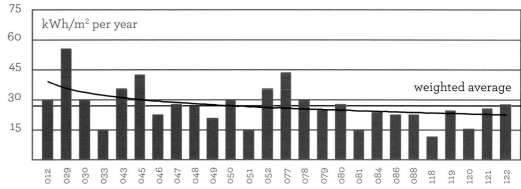

RENOVATION OF COLLECTIVE HOUSING: NET HEATING REQUIREMENT

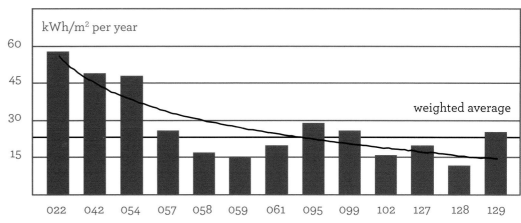

Renovating a listed house on Avenue Ducpétiaux [077]: the engineering design work to improve the insulation and airtightness of the existing window frames led to a second series of matching frames fitted on the inside, a solution endorsed by the Royal Commission for Monuments and Sites, even if it could not be applied to the most complex frames (S. Closson, architect).

IN THE OWNER'S WORDS

"We could have envisaged doing the work in phases, but it would have complicated things for certain delicate interventions such as the sealing or the inside insulation of the front façade", says Benjamin Clarysse [122]. "This would have extended the working period, estimated at six months."

09/ ANTICIPATE A PHASED RENOVATION

The important thing is that all work done today can permit, both technically and economically, these renovations to be further improved later, to enable all buildings to evolve towards "almost zero energy".

Even if a building can be renovated immediately to this level, the renovation will have value only if it allows a subsequent renovation – the upgrade– taking the building further on the path to energy independence.

This is the principle applied for the Rue Huberti [051]: a three-stage renovation, from what exists to low energy ($BEN_{ch} \leq 60$ kWh / m²), then very low energy ($BEN_{ch} \leq 30$ kWh / m²) and finally passive ($BEN_{ch} \leq 15$ kWh /m²). This principle made it possible to gradually raise the necessary funds and take full advantage of the premiums and subsidies on offer.

The renovation plan has taken care to ensure that each investment does not get in the way of the subsequent work. Phase 1 was to insulate the floors and the roof, to improve the sealing of the building and install double flow mechanical ventilation. The existing heating installation was replaced by a condensation boiler, reducing energy costs by 40%. Phase 2 allowed the house to achieve a low energy level of 28 kWh/m² per year by insulating the rear façade and replacing the existing joinery. Phase 3, aimed at the 15 kWh/m² passive standard, involved insulating the front façade, replacing the final joinery and installing sunscreens.

When all was said and done, Rue Huberti's owners [051] opted not to live for years in a building site and the house is, already today, renovated to passive level.

Such a roadmap, drawn from a simplified audit, should guide all sustainable renovation: do nothing today that cannot be put to good use tomorrow. Indeed, a renovation will be cost-effective tomorrow only if it does not require the demolition of that which was done yesterday: even if it means changing the frames, it is better to give oneself the possibility of insulating the façade from the outside. To improve the durability of technical installations, it is important to make them easily accessible and ensure that they are maintained.

Let's not be dogmatic. For me, my project, I will admit, gave me a lot of pleasure..."

condensation boiler as a booster, with the idea of moving at a later stage to low temperature heating: "We knew that, beyond that, we would have to touch the walls in order to insulate the building correctly, involving a renovation in greater depth. At the time, we were not talking passive."

Little by little, Olivier immersed himself in the emerging thinking on passive housing. "The passive pioneers had such a desire to share and have other people discover what they were experimenting that it ended up rubbing off on me as well." With the help of a specialized engineering office (Ecorce), Olivier decided to push his renovation project as far as possible. He therefore introduced his dossier at the second call for "Exemplary buildings" projects (Batex 2008).

the building site called for a more radical approach to controlling costs. It began with careful negotiation with a carefully selected and very committed general contractor – "Word of mouth is starting to operate here, including through Batex calls for projects." Olivier quickly understood that it was better to keep his general contractor away from very specialized items, such as ventilation or airtightness, which would lead him to inflate his prices to provide a safety margin for those tasks his team did not yet master adequately. "There are also some items requiring particular care and one can do oneself, with a better outcome and lower cost, providing you devote the necessary time to them."

This gently reduces the budget. Moreover, when it comes to financing such expenditures, not all bankers are equally receptive. Here it was necessary to renegotiate the twenty-five year mortgage contract with a bank sensitive to passive housing and eco-renovation, a process which provided considerable additional resources, enabling the exercise to be pushed very far. Probably too far for common or garden renovators, Olivier is ready to admit. But nor does he dismiss the pleasure of living in a house with a vocation today to inspire other exemplary renovation projects.

Youth centre, Chaussée d'Anvers [001]: the L'Avenir youth centre places a light-weight structure on the concrete base of an existing supermarket lying at the foot of the housing tower blocks of the Chaussée d'Anvers. Made entirely from FSC timber with good insulation in cellulose (K20), it also has an extensive green roof (a courtesy to the occupants of the neighbouring towers) and a planted curtain wall (R²D² architecture).

INHABITED CITY
AMENITIES INCLUDED

A city is composed not only of homes: it is a centre of economic activities which, following the departure of the industrial sector, focus mainly on services and knowledge. Certain of these accompany the inhabitants during their daily life: nurseries, schools and youth or health centres, hospitals and residences for the elderly, cultural centres, places of worship, sporting facilities, etc.

AMENITIES AND SUSTAINABLE CONSTRUCTION

100 % have reinforced insulation
100 % use double flow ventilation
96 % have installed solar protection systems or a passive cooling system
89 % have installed a cistern or are managing rain water on their plots
83 % use mostly eco- materials
77 % have converted their premises for easy bike use
75 % use solar thermal and/or photovoltaic panels
67 % have planted all or part of their roof

Passive Gaucheret nursery, Rue Rogier [004]: the building has a wood frame in fully FSC-labelled wood. Particular attention has been paid to the environmental impact of the finishing materials (MDW architecture).

Renovation of the Brasseries Belle-Vue [112]: renovation into a high-performance building complex is achieved mainly by the internal insulation of the main building, enabling it to reach a low energy level. The double-flow ventilation is supplemented with passive cooling by adiabatic humidification (A2M architectes).

Saint-Pierre University Hospital [072] and the Brugmann Traumatology and Rehabilitation Centre [076]: the new wing of the Saint-Pierre University Hospital and the Brugmann Centre extension attain net heating needs of 8 to 8.4 kWh/m²/year, well beyond the passive criteria… (Bureau d'Architecture E. Verhaegen; Hoet+Minne, société d'architectes).

The Brussels "demographic shock" entails major implications regarding educational, cultural, sports and other civic amenities. The Brussels statistics institute[1] (Institut bruxellois de Statistiques) expects an additional 32 500 pupils by 2020 and estimates a need for 79 new schools by 2015. This is quite a challenge.

The first four editions of Batex awarded 40 amenities projects with a surface area of almost 112 000 m², including 30% under renovation. Furthermore, 11 other mixed projects include a small amenities part in programmes for homes or offices. With work on 30% of the Batex areas under way, the amenities sector is receiving over EUR 8 million, representing 35% of the grants.

The sector of healthcare and assistance to the elderly takes the lion's share, with six projects amounting to about half the surface areas involved. A third quarter is shared by sixteen nurseries, ten schools and eight cultural amenities. The last quarter is divided between three projects for hotels, the renovation of a gymasium and that of the Laeken Baths [145].

[1] *Cahiers de l'IBSA n° 2: Impact de l'essor démographique sur la population scolaire en Région de Bruxelles-Capitale* (2010) (Impact of the demographic growth on the school population in the Brussels-Capital Region).

01/ COMPLETED PROJECTS

Projects for amenities are those that take longest to mature. Most of them are still under way and six buildings have been completed to date: the Avenir Youth Centre [001] in Brussels, the Gaucheret nursery [004] at Schaerbeek and the Saint-François nursery [071] at Saint-Josse-ten-Noode, the IMMI secondary school [023] at Anderlecht, the antenna of the SIAMU (Service d'Incendie et d'Aide Médicale Urgente – Fire Brigade and Emergency Medical Service) [038] at Schaerbeek and the Malibran Community Centre [039].

The Rue Saint-François nursery brings to thirteen the number of nurseries that have adopted the passive standard. Most of these take advantage of renewable energy sources via solar thermal collectors. They all have well-designed insulation systems (K15 to K23) and double flow ventilation.

Fourteen nurseries recover rainwater and twelve now have a planted roof. They all pay special attention to the children's health and thus to the choice of environmentally friendly materials free of any harmful components.

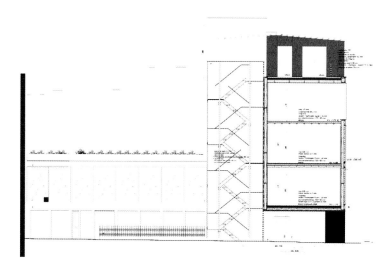

[BATEX 071– THE RUE SAINT-FRANÇOIS NURSERY][1]

Rue Saint-François 34-36 at 1210 Saint-Josse-ten-Noode | Commune de Saint-Josse-ten-Noode | 02 société d'architectes | Label-A

PLAYFUL LOCAL ARCHITECTURE

Opposite the Saint-Josse-ten-Noode swimming pool, the O2[2] architects delivered a nursery in 2011 with 30 beds and 3 apartments, following a competition organised as part of the Méridien Quarter Contract.

This was a team operation bringing together engineers and architects with the In Advance firm, which was acting as the contracting authority under delegation from the Municipality. This kind of operation has the advantage of establishing the specifications in advance, along with the details and – last but not least – the costs.

ECOLOGY OF URBAN DENSITY
The context is extremely dense and the particular 'island' is a very built-up area, so the project had to free up land in order to create a garden for the children and allow the best possible access for natural light, as well as creating a lasting and passive construction. All this work continues with a green area on two levels (the planted roofs), providing a degree of relief in the very 'mineral' surroundings.

DETACHING STRUCTURE FROM THE ENVELOPE
Taking their distance from the surrounding buildings, the architects opted for a concrete structure, which gives the construction rigidity and inertia. They completed it with wood frame walls assembled and insulated on site. Airtightness was achieved mainly by coffering and, in order to neutralise air leakage between the flats (without any thermal consequence), the three flats were tested simultaneously by a blower door. The nursery requires 13 kWh/m² net per year and the flats between 6 and 12 kWh/m².

EXTERNAL CIRCULATION
To give people with reduced mobility access to the flats, the building was equipped with a lift, situated outside the building, along with the staircase, in order to reduce the heated volume and simplify ventilation and fire safety requirements.

SUNSCREEN WITH HIGH PRIVACY COEFFICIENT
Since the nursery and the flats have living spaces that receive a great deal of sunlight and are oriented towards the interior of the island, the bedrooms and rest areas face the road, where large perforated sunscreen panels slide from one facade to another. Although they face north, they are still useful to protect the privacy of the homes in a very narrow street. The same concern is addressed by the metal mesh that protects the external staircase in the island. On the sun side, the system reaches the height of playfulness and its variations in solar mode project sparkling patches, which, over the nursery day area, create the effect of a giant hopscotch area for the toddlers.

This use of sunlight is reflected inside by a colour scheme dominated by yellow and green.

[1] Read the report in *be.passive* 09, October 2011, p. 37 ff.
[2] www.02-architectures.org

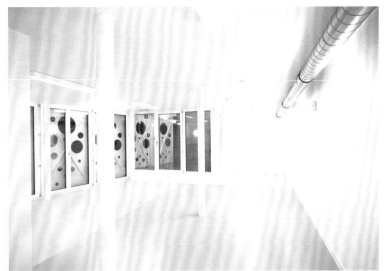

Renovation of an office building on Rue Montoyer [107]: complete insulation of the building, with reduction of thermal bridges, makes it possible to approach 20kWh/m²/year or almost passive, like these offices, which also benefit from high compactness (ARTE POLIS).

02/ HUNTING FOR DRAFTS

The energy quality of a building depends on the absence of drafts caused by construction defects – cracks, defective joints, etc. – which are bothersome and cause significant energy losses.

They are also likely to cause damage through condensation in the walls. Whatever the type of ventilation used (natural or mechanical), these parasite losses must be controlled.

Hunting for air leaks is a new branch of work for companies, which must be trained and equipped for this. This test for airtightness – also known as the "n50" or the "blower door®" test – is carried out on completion of the closed structural work, before the finishing work. It is performed using a ventilator to create a 50 Pascal pressure difference between the interior of the building and the exterior. This makes it possible to check whether the air loss from the various leaks is acceptable and, if necessary, to correct it. The points of attention for the airtightness of housing have been studied by the BBRI[1] and by Bruxelles Environnement[2].

In concrete terms, companies can achieve this airtightness using traditional means such as plastering or by employing sealing membranes fixed to the construction joints, for example between a window frame and the wall.The candidates themselves fix the level of airtightness to be achieved. In passive architecture, it will conform to the criterion of 0.6 renewal per hour. The selection of initial results given below (some of which are intermediate measures) show that most targets were achieved.

Since they could not assess the airtightness of their buildings after renovation before work started, certain award-winners simply used the default value (n50 = 7.8 vol/h) and had little difficulty in reducing it to 1.5 or even 0.95, as in the case of Chaussée de Forest [046]. Other renovation work was more complex, as in the case of Rue Vanpé [014] or Avenue Ducpétiaux [077], because their listed facades cannot be modified. The workshop of the Nos Pilifs [011] farm did not manage to achieve 0.6 vol/h because of a large garage door that was not airtight enough.

The relatively disappointing intermediate result for the Loi 42 project [068] is due particularly to the experimental use of a prefabrication procedure that did not distinguish between the walls that had to be airtight and the others. The corrections that needed to be made on the site turned out to be more difficult than foreseen, even though the n50 value has now been almost achieved[3].

[1] CSTC-Contact n°33 (1/2012), *L'étanchéité à l'air des bâtiments : un défi majeur pour l'ensemble des corps de métier*, Centre Scientifique et Technique de la Construction, www.cstc.be > Publications > CSTC-Contact
[2] Fiches 1.1 et 1.2 : L'étanchéité à l'air (2010); www.bruxellesenvironnement.be > Particuliers > Thèmes > Eco-construction > Nos info-fiches.
[3] See *be.passive* 10, January 2012, p. 37.

AIRTIGHTNESS: TARGETS AND MEASUREMENTS BY BLOWER-DOOR; RENOVATION AND NEW

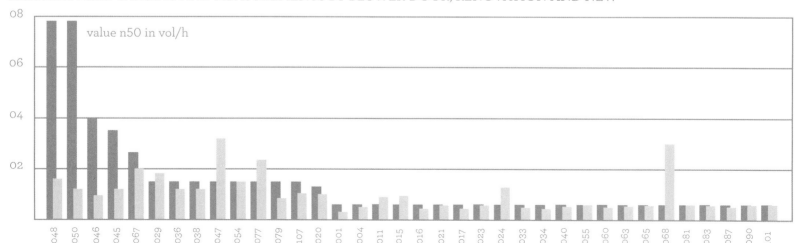

value n50 in vol/h

Renovation and heightening of a building on Rue de la Loi [068]: the architects used a prefabrication method which unfortunately did not distinguish walls needing to be airtight from the other walls. Corrections had to be made on site, which proved more difficult than planned, even if the n50 value is nearly reached today (Synergy international).

A CONTRACTOR'S EXPERIENCE

Our first experience of the blower door® test was complicated. It involved a five-storey building with a concrete structure and a coffered facade in insulated wood and sealing membranes, with small flats and an outside staircase [Rue Saint-François nursery, 071]. The first results when we tested each unit separately were very disappointing because of leaks between the flats (ducts, etc.). Passive architecture requires a new approach on the building site. Small, badly finished details badly distorted the overall result. However, with the cooperation of everyone involved on the site, the final result was absolutely positive. At the Neerstalle site [096], we chose to do the airproofing from the inside using traditional plastering."

Olivier Renier,
contractor In Advance [071] [096]

BLOWER DOOR®, N50 AND AIRTIGHTNESS METRICS

These barbaric names indicate the procedure to follow in order to establish the level of airtightness in a building. In passive architecture, the requirement is a reading of 0.6 vol/h at 50 Pa: this means that during the test, which sets up a 50 Pa pressure difference (the equivalent of a storm wind) between the interior and the exterior, only 60% of the interior air volume will be renewed over one hour.

AMENITIES
AND ENERGY NEEDS

Net heating needs – new construction,
average: 18.4 kWh/m² per year

Net heating needs – renovation,
average: 35.4 kWh/m² per year

Polyclinic on Rue de la Cible [015]: the CPAS/OCMW manages to cover 60% of its water needs with a 100 000 litre tank, while 33% of sanitary hot water needs are provided by solar thermal panels (separate solar tanks facilitate heat treatment to prevent legionellosis) (ETAU).

Fire and Emergency Medical Service (SIAMU), Chaussée d'Haecht [038]: with the SIAMU outpost at Schaerbeek containing fire truck garages, only the occupied portion meets the high airtightness and insulation standards (K22) (Hoet, Minne, Arcoplan consortium).

03/ AMENITIES AND ENERGY

The various Batex amenities have an average net heating need (BEN_{ch}) of 23.4 kWh/m² per year; in new buildings, this falls to 18.4 kWh/m²; in renovated buildings, it rises to 35.4 kWh/m² per year.

Together, they will make an annual saving of over 1 050 000 litres of fuel. If we take into account only savings on heating, the present increase in energy costs and the price of 0.90 €/l, the Batex subsidies represent less than 6 years of functioning.

NET HEATING REQUIREMENT 2007-2011 RENOVATION OF COLLECTIVE AMENITIES

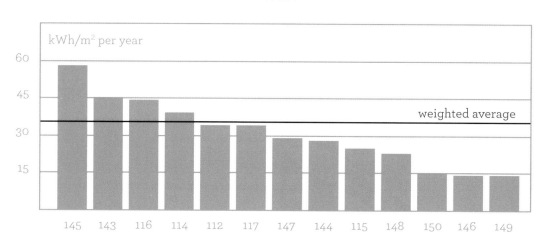

kWh/m² per year

weighted average

145 143 116 114 112 117 147 144 115 148 150 146 149

NET HEATING REQUIREMENT 2007-2011 CONSTRUCTION OF COLLECTIVE AMENITIES

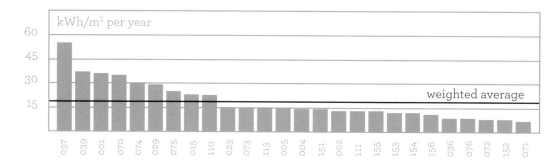

kWh/m² per year

weighted average

037 039 001 070 074 029 075 015 110 023 073 113 005 004 151 002 111 155 153 154 156 036 076 072 152 071

Pierre Somers,
architect

[TESTIMONY]

THE ENTHUSIASM OF THE DESIGNERS IN A HARD SCHOOL
THE IMMI SCHOOL [023]

What is the point in designing a building that is exemplary in terms of energy saving and environmental friendliness if its occupants do whatever they fancy?
In this school at Anderlecht, the rigour of the designers constantly has to come to terms with the bad habits of the users. But after all, that's how people learn, isn't it?

"In a school, regulation requires some schooling – and someone who is really interested in taking charge of it… That's the big challenge for full performance in passive building."

It is the morning break between lessons. It is bitterly cold now in early February; for ten days the thermometer has been at -15°C. A handful of pupils are occupying the the entrance hall of the new building designed according to passive standards, shamelessly letting the winter wind rush in through the corridors When, by dint of coming and going, it slyly insinuates its way into the classrooms, someone is bound to complain: "It's unbelievable, we were promised a Rolls Royce low energy building and now, at the slightest hint of frost, we are freezing in the classrooms!"

Pierre Somers, the architect (TRAIT Architects) who designed this new "exemplary" project, takes it philosophically: he knows that, as in most school buildings, people are more used to patched-up buildings than to brand new amenities, especially if they are hi tech. You need time to convince people: "Regarding sustainable building, a school is the ideal customer because it does not have the means to build cheaply in a short term perspective. If it installs provisional containers which will cost it a fortune to heat, which will gradually cause the pupils to flee and which in a few years will have to be replaced in any case, it is blocking its own future. On this basis, our demonstration can gradually lead the customer to opt for sustainable, low energy buildings."

Somers set to work as soon as the offer was accepted. He proposed a low energy design with automatic ventilation, lighting that reacts to daylight, solutions to collect rainwater and transform it into drinking water by reverse osmosis and ecological building methods. Each time, he argued that if all these features slightly exceeded the very tight budget imposed on the establishment, the costs would soon be covered, with greater comfort and gradual savings that can be invested in teaching projects. "A building site lasts for about one year and in the life of a pupil it is very meaningful. It is also an excellent opportunity to communicate positive messages in terms of the environment."

However, Somers has had plenty of experience with schools and he knows that the performance will depend on the manner in which his finely constructed tool is put to use: "The PO, the school's managers, the teaching staff: these are all different people with different opinions. Some will be convinced, others not at all, and they all have direct power over the day-to-day building, so there are bound to be some misunderstandings."

Here too, he takes a philosophical approach: "You can have a high performance car and use it accordingly, or else stay in first gear and drive at 15 miles an hour on the motorway, using up all the fuel and putting the engine at risk. I designed this as a very comfortable, high performance building. It still needs to be well regulated and supervised: this is the role of maintenance. It also needs to be used well, and this depends exclusively on its occupants. If one of these ingredients is lacking, it is bound to be less of a pleasant, high performance building than was promised. However, at least, the infrastructure was created to achieve this goal, rapidly or by gradually incorporating the teaching it gives you on the degree of attainable performance and the savings that can derive from it. It is true that this requires enhanced awareness and changes in behaviour. However, that is bound to be better than continuing to build energy sieves that entail ever increasing energy charges over the coming years!"

Showing that the message is beginning to get through, the PO has decided to continue passive renovation of another school building and the board of directors has opened an "environmental management" section.

[BATEX 023– THE IMMI SCHOOL] [1]

Avenue des Résédas 51 at 1070 Anderlecht | IMMI asbl | TRAIT architects sa | Ecorce, Atelier Chora

TEACHING BY EXAMPLE

Situated in the heart of the La Roue neighbourhood in Anderlecht, Brussels' first passive school is a 1515 m² building, delivered in 2009 by the Trait architects' practice for the Institute of Mary Immaculate – Montjoie in replacement of a very old school building at the back of an antiquated architectural patchwork typical of all school systems.

It includes a dining hall and its kitchen, 10 classrooms, toilets and service rooms on three floors.

Open to the south-east, the project is built against a high party wall. The classrooms receive excellent light, corrected by a wide overhang of the roof; the school is a long building with 5 classrooms arranged in series on each floor, and each classroom is supplied with fresh air via the ventilation ducts placed in the corridors.

INERTIA FOR STABLE COMFORT

The building has a heavy concrete structure covered in wood coffering made of TJI composite beams and insulated with flaked cellulose and hemp wool. The whole structure is covered with wood cladding. The support structure and the walls are made airtight by glued membranes. The situation in the interior of a densely built-up 'island' rendered access to the site difficult, especially for the delivery of prefabricated elements.

TEACHING BY USE

Heating requirements are reduced to 15 kWh/m² per year, in conformity with the passive standard. For IMMI, this represents a tenfold reduction in operating costs. The ventilation, the solar protection systems and the lighting are controlled by a powerful regulation system with presence detectors. The solar protection systems are combined with a nocturnal ventilation system to reduce any overheating risk. The fact that these control systems are automatic does not, however, completely release the users from their responsibility: as in every new building, its proper functioning relies on correct use. Seen in this way, it is a fully pedagogical building!

50% of the hot water supply to the toilets is provided by thermal solar captors. The school collects rainwater and transforms part of it into drinking water. Taps with flow restriction, dual flush toilets and automatic flushing urinals have been installed. The institute wishes to extend this new relationship to water via an educational pond project.

A WISE INVESTMENT

Schools have tight budgets. The project estimated the added cost of the passive standard as 11% in 2007 and the return on the investment was assessed as 10-15 years on the basis of a heating fuel price of 0.55 €/l without taking premiums into account. At the end of the day, this is what influenced the decision by school's directors, who no doubt have no regrets now that fuel prices have risen to 0.90 €/l !

[1] See be.passive 09, October 2011, p. 37 ff.

04/ THE EXPERIENCE OF THE FIRST PASSIVE SCHOOLS

The experience of the first schools has confirmed their efficiency in reducing the main factors of their energy footprint.

"For a school, it is the heating, so it is worth while investing energy and money in this direction", explains engineer Lionel Wauters[1]. "Furthermore, passive architecture with its controlled ventilation provides excellent air quality and avoids carbon dioxide peaks which lower pupils' attention[2]. This is ideal for a school." However, considerable attention must be given to improving control of natural and artificial lighting and that of the ventilation (which must be able to be switched off outside school hours). Also, every effort must be made to reduce the task of managing the building via simple systems.

A follow-up mission must be arranged to make sure the equipment is correctly regulated. First of all, however, the right contact person must be found: "In a school, regulation requires some schooling – and someone who is really interested in taking charge of it!", comments Pierre Somers[3]. "At present it is difficult to find specialised technical engineers who are not excessively fascinated by complexity and who are willing to admit that, in certain cases, simplicity is far preferable to complicated solutions that are impenetrable for users and often very expensive. If I had to start all over again, I would do exactly the same, with the exception of the regulation, for which I would choose much simpler components with, for example, a small radiator in each classroom."

When renovation is difficult, other tools are available to schools. Not only was the Avenue Montjoie project [148] the Batex 2011 award winner, it is also part of the P.L.A.G.E. programme, and each year the monitoring of heating, electricity and water consumption will be performed by a pupil as part of his or her end of studies project.

[1] See be.passive 03, March 2010, p. 38.
[2] Jacques Claessens, "Équipements pour une école passive", be.passive 10 and 11, 2012.
[3] See his interview in be.passive 11, face-à-face, p. 18.

Passive BSKA school, Avenue Edmond Mesens [111]: the project is based on an integrated approach to sustainable development that focuses on social, spatial, energy and ecological criteria. It is part of the Flemish Ministry of Education's programme to build 25 passive schools (EVR-Architecten).

Passive BSKA school, Avenue Edmond Mesens [111]: the volume is designed to both achieve heat savings in winter and limit cooling costs in summer while remaining welcoming and accessible (EVR-Architecten).

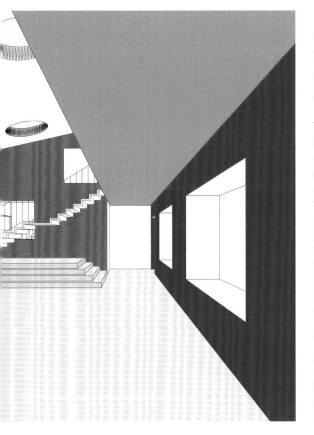

05/ PROJECTS UNDER WAY

Two other new school projects are under construction (Place Emile Bockstael [002] at Laeken and the BS KA school [111] at Etterbeek) and a fourth school, Arts & Métiers [154], is being planned. Batex has also accepted six renovation projects.

Three of these – Ulens [114], Chazal [147] and Montjoie [148] –, achieve the low or very low energy level. The others will achieve the passive standard, fully in the case of the renovation and extension of the Simons project school [137] and that of Merchtem [150], which is rebuilding its entire external envelope; partially for the Rousseau project [149] in which the renovation involves the extension of the building with a new passive volume on the roof of the existing building. The project to renovate a school on Avenue Chazal [147] takes particularly ingenious advantage of the constraints of the existing building.

The Batex hospital projects show that major progress is possible. The project for the PSAC of Saint-Josse-ten-Noode on Rue de la Cible [015] involves renovating the Polyclinic and building a retirement home with 148 individual rooms. It has a net heating need of 23 kWh/m² per year and controls its electrical air conditioning needs via a night cooling strategy for the polyclinic and the use of a ventilated space in the basement as a 'Canadian well' ground-coupled heat exchanger for the retirement home.

The Brugmann University Hospital [036], the new wing of the Saint-Pierre University Hospital [072] and the extension of the traumatology centre of the Brugmann Hospital [076] at Laeken have an energy need of 8 to 8.4 kWh/m². The La Cerisaie medicalised retirement home [037] and the new antenna of the SIAMU (Service d'Incendie et d'Aide Médicale Urgente or Fire Brigade and Emergency Medical Service) [038] are large buildings that are compact by nature. Le Clos de la Quiétude [075] was able to reduce its net heating needs to 25 kWh/m² per year, particularly because of its highly compact structure and the use of very efficient insulating materials!

Renovation of a sports centre on Rue du Sceptre [144]: this project reconstructs a large 500 m² gymnasium, with flexibility provided by the lack of columns. Energy-wise, the project reduces the net heating need to 28 kWh/m²/year through insulation, sealing, compactness and good window orientation (P. Blondel, architect).

Place Willems [152]: the two-storey passive nursery is built on a base which includes all the public and technical spaces. The project is based essentially on the use of wood for the structure, insulation and facing (Trait, Norrenberg & Somers Architectes).

The passive nursery in the Rue du Guldem Bodem [005]: the envelope was designed to minimize energy losses and unwanted heat intake. An intensive green roof was planned, while rainwater is also recovered from the next-door roof (A2M architectes).

Several projects should be starting soon, such as the HOPPA project (Hébergement Occupationnel pour Personnes Polyhandicapées Adultes – Occupational Residential Centre for Adults with Multiple Handicaps) at Berchem-Sainte-Agathe [074], two buildings to house 15 autistic people for the non-profit organisation Coupole bruxelloise de l'Autisme [110] at Jette and the project to build flats for people suffering from various mental handicaps at Rue du Wimpelberg [155] for the non-profit organisation Le Potelier.

Another project that has been selected is the renovation of the Community Centre [143], situated between adjoining buildings in a densely built-up island: it is part of the Navez-Portaels Neighbourhood Contract at Schaerbeek.

The municipality of Jette is studying another public project, the construction of a funeral home [070] with an FSC certified timber frame insulated by cellulose and wood fibre. An ambitious project is the renovation of the De Rinck cultural centre [115], a group of buildings with a surface area of 2 793 m² right in the centre of Anderlecht.

As for the private projects, an all-glass art gallery between the road and the garden will be built on the ground floor on Rue du Pépin [062]. Finally, the passive project for the Kouba mosque [156], will be built at Schaerbeek for the non-profit organisation ACIRSP.

In 2011, Batex selected its first sports amenities projects: the renovation of the gymnasium on Rue du Sceptre at Ixelles [144] and that of the swimming baths of Laeken [145]. At Laeken, the project involves the energy renovation of a group of buildings housing two swimming pools and gymnasiums. At Ixelles, the project [144] is part of the Sceptre sustainable Neighbourhood Contract. It gives the sports complex new visibility by working on its lateral facade along the railway line (where a footpath will be constructed) and by reorganising all the roofs (which will be planted).

The last major amenities, still in the project stage, are hotels. Two projects for passive hotels and a low energy renovation project were selected in 2009 and 2011. The conversion of the former Belle-Vue brewery [112] into a hotel complex with 150 rooms is under way at present.

The Atlantis concept [113] is even more original: the original floating hotel has been transformed into a youth hostel. It will be moored alongside the canal on a floating concrete foundation. The "unplugged" comfort of the 60 passive rooms will be provided by the usual strategies of insulation, airtightness and ventilation.

Finally, the malthouse of the Belle-Vue brewery, bought by the municipality of Molenbeek-Saint-Jean, will be renovated to provide multipurpose areas completed by a new Quai du Hainaut hotel (a new construction) [140]. The Municipality wants to make this its flagship, thereby promoting "green" tourism.

Passive hotel and cultural amenities on the Quai du Hainaut [140]: this part of the former Belle-Vue breweries will be renovated to the low energy standard and a new 29 room hotel built to the passive standard in a concrete frame enveloped in cellulose-insulated wood caissons (L'Escaut-MSA-Grontmij consortium).

"I cannot imagine constructing or renovating a building nowadays without looking far ahead into the future to espy the developments our society is waiting for, without trying to contribute to this future that is taking shape before our very eyes. An exemplary building is also a tool, that everyone can see, for changing mentalities."

Béa Diallo, the former boxing champion who is now an alderman (for family, youth, employment, social integration, relations between the generations and equal opportunities) at Ixelles, is infectiously enthusiastic. His project of integration through sport, Emergence, inspired by a project of the same name successfully developed at Le Havre, has already convinced the Brussels Region to finance the renovation of an abandoned former industrial warehouse and its transformation into a gymnasium and fitness centre open to all, alongside training areas. "The Brussels Capital Region was interested in my project because in their area over 35% of young people aged between eighteen and thirty-five are unemployed. The idea was to use boxing and sport in general to reach underqualified young people with no diplomas or professional experience whom the classic local structures are unable to attract, and to offer them sporting activities together with access to training schemes. They will not all have to get into the boxing ring, but they will be shown the work involved in training a boxing champion. We want to tell them that they may feel strong in the street because they do as they like but that if they want to enter a boxing ring and hold their own they need to put in work and respect rules. Otherwise, they will get nowhere. It is the same in life. It is essentially a combat in which there are steps to take and rules that must be respected."

For those who are hooked and are particularly keen to enter the fray, he also offers training modules called "At the top for a job" with internships in companies. It works! Most of the first candidates have found a job. Of course, it is also true that our hero has taken the trouble to get managing directors to occupy over half the places on his board of directors.

To go further still, Diallo needed a place, a gymnasium that would attract his protégés: fitness, boxing, martial arts, body-building etc., but also a place of well-being with a sauna and a Turkish bath. Not a run-down hovel, as is so often the case, at the end of a cul-de-sac. What he wanted was a place that really functioned, modern, well lit and comfortable. It had to be a place looking the future straight in the eye. The transformation of this abandoned building beside the Namur to Luxembourg railway line was just right because it was very visible: "I cannot imagine constructing or renovating a building nowadays without looking far ahead into the future to espy the developments our society is waiting for, without trying to contribute to this future that is taking shape before our very eyes. An exemplary building is also a tool that everyone can see, for changing mentalities. For a municipality, it is a duty to show an example on this level."

His gamble also involves the attraction that such a structure, well equipped and easily accessible, can have on neighbourhood residents regardless of their origin or age – sport tends to iron out differences – to create a link. He does, however, recognise that "responding to this call for projects has complicated things a bit and put the brakes on my plans. But what are these little drawbacks beside the example it gives to young people and to the residents of this neighbourhood?"

WORKING PLACES

[CHAPTER 06]

The Brussels urban fabric meshes economic activity with residential areas and amenities. In Brussels, the service sector accounts for around 92% of jobs, with the other 8% in the secondary sector (mainly manufacturing and building) [1]. Naturally, Batex reflects this specific context: with only 25 award-winning projects, the places of work sites nevertheless account for 38% of surface area under construction and 31% of grants.

[1] Mini-Bru 2012, Institut bruxellois de Statistiques et d'Analyse, 2011 edition.

Renovation of listed offices on Boulevard de l'Impératrice [006]: Telex is restoring a heritage jewel of the post-war period located in the city centre and well served by public transport. The project reduces its heating need to 71 kWh/m²/year. A photovoltaic system produces 6 000 kWh per year (Crepain Binst Architecture).

We are speaking of a surface area of over 140 000 m², leaving aside small office areas included in housing programmes. This includes very small projects such as the 156 m² of offices for the Energy Counter on Rue du Fort [106] and more ambitious ones such as the 7 500 m² of the Aéropolis passive offices [040] or the construction of a passive office block of around 20 000 m² on Rue Belliard [142]. In addition to offices there are a carpentry workshop on Rue Faes [008], maintenance premises for the Nos Pilifs farm [011], the large Caméléon sales counter [025], the refrigerators for the Mabru morning market [069] and the renovation of the former Byrrh industrial building [139]. 40% of the office projects involve renovation.

The Batex figures include third sector activities (75%), commercial activities (12%) and industrial ones (13%). After the record opening year of 66 000 m² in 2007, the surfaces came back down to 20 000 m² in 2008 and 15 000 m² in 2009, before increasing once more to 50 000 m² in 2011, corresponding to 12% of new occupancies on the market.

Renovation of listed offices on
Boulevard de l'Impératrice
[006]: strict compliance with
existing elevations has
led Telex to develop a second
'active' glazed skin, integrating
mechanical ventilation
and solar protection, which
also improves the acoustic
comfort of the offices (Crepain
Binst Architecture).

Renovation of an office building
on Rue Montoyer [107]: this
operation to upgrade offices
dating from the sixties is also
aimed (in addition to Batex) at
obtaining BREEAM certification
(ARTE POLIS).

01/ A VOLATILE SECTOR

The Brussels office market is very specific: over the years, promoters have maintained a dynamic whereby new buildings go rapidly out of date[1], with new offices being rented or sold more cheaply than existing facilities.

However, the crisis has hit this floor space-producing machine – and the building waste it creates. The bubble has burst, and the market has ground to a halt with vacancies of over 33% in the outskirts and 9% in Brussels itself[2]. This represents an overall area of over 1 190 000 m²! This is not really the ideal context for building new traditional areas and the players are forced to reflect on the potential for renovation and the location of projects. There must be a reason for the fact that three Batex projects[3] launched in 2007 with an overall area of 22 000 m² are still awaiting investors! "Nowadays", explains Eric De Keuleneer, the award-winning project owner for Loi 42 [068], "in many large towns, the value of a high performance office block in terms of energy or the environment possesses an added value over and above the strict energy saving. It possesses ethical elements, and certain occupants refuse to rent a property that does not correspond to these environmental features."

A form of green certification may be looked for to "make the difference" against competitors. In the view of promoter Sophie Le Clercq, Batex 2007 gave a form of certification to her project at Avenue Van Volxem [032] "We are looking more for publicity, a label, a reputation associated with the quality of the project[4]." Other projects, such as the Science-Montoyer offices [107] or Quai Léon Monnoyer [141], hope to obtain the BREEAM label[5] (as well as Batex). Numerous seminars are organised on this subject and designers and investors are continuing their reflection on the future of environmentally friendly offices. Here, Batex functions as a laboratory.

[1] Christian Lasserre, "Economie du projet durable : Bruxelles et ses bureaux", in Eco-logiques: les bénéfices de l'approche environnementale, Les Cahiers de La Cambre Architecture n°4, La Lettre Volée, 2005.
[2] Observatoire des bureaux, Vacance 2011 à Bruxelles, SDRB, http://urbanisme.irisnet.be/actualites-accueil/pdf/lobservatoire-des-bureaux-ndeg29
[3] These are the following projects: Galilei [027], Van Volxem [032] and Clémenceau [041].
[4] Vert Bruxelles! Architectures à suivre, Racine, 2009, p. 47 and 91.
[5] British Research Establishment Environmental Assessment Method: environmental certification of buildings delivered by the British Building Science Centre, www.breeam.org
[6] BSBC (Flemish Region), the Eco-Build Cluster (Brussels Capital Region) and the Eco-Construction Cluster (Walloon Region).

Passive offices on Avenue Urbain Britsiers [040]: the building meets the best criteria of comfort and management demanded by a European clientele, but with clearly reduced electricity and heating consumption, enabling the owners to recover the 4% additional cost over 5 years (Architectes Associés).

02/ NEWLY BUILT BATEX OFFICES

Large offices permit global approaches. If the model is robust at the outset, it will adapt to the specific character of the place, of the programme or of the customer without losing its inherent logic.

In 2007, this model was not the passive standard. Some people even believed this was quite unsuited to the sector. The first Batex projects first looked for an alternative to passive architecture, with Van Volxem [032] and Clémenceau [041], which used geothermic technology and thermally activated concrete slabs, but these projects never came to fruition.

The Elia offices [020] belonged to this pre-passive generation and benefited from significant heat gains related to their installation of computer servers to reduce the need for heating to a very respectable 18 kWh/m² per year, while meeting demanding standards of comfort. Drawing lessons from this initial Batex project, the Elia company has now opened a second Batex worksite, Monnoyer [141], which will be passive or even zero energy!

THE PASSIVE
CRITERIA IN
A COMMERCIAL BUILDING

(1) Net heating need:
≤ 15 kWh/m² per year [1]
(2) Net cooling need:
≤ 15 kWh/m² per year
(3) Primary energy (calculated
for heating, cooling, lighting and
auxiliary equipment): PE ≤ 90 – 2.5 x
compactness [2] (kWh/m² per year)
(4) Airtightness: the rate of air
change is ≤ 0.6 vol/h (measured at a
difference of 50 Pascal).
(5) Risk of overheating: the comfort
level is consistent with Belgian standard NBN 15251 and the overheating
percentage (T > 25°C) is ≤ 5%.

A Vademecum is a downloadable
from www.maisonpassive.be

03/ ONCE UPON A TIME THERE WAS PASSIVE BUILDING

All the other new Batex office projects have been designed to the passive standard. But it is important to realize that the passive standard was originally conceived for residential buildings. The energy conception of office building is very different in terms of type of occupation and amenities.

The large glazed surfaces also generate a lot of heat. The main concern here is not heating (as in residential building), but cooling. It was long feared that further insulating offices (for winter) would make them even more prone to overheating (in summer). The results show that this is not so – providing that the design is based on bioclimatic principles.

Lighting, on the other hand, accounts for 30-50% of energy consumption in commercial buildings, while it is marginal in residential building. Good architectural design needs to take advantage of natural light, complementing it with a strategy of sun protection and of control of the artificial lighting [3]. In this context it can make sense to reduce the distance between opposite walls – thereby making the project less compact – as at Marly [065] or Monnoyer [141].

[1] Equivalent to 1.5 litres of oil per square metre per year.
[2] The compactness is the ratio of gross building volume to its heat loss surface. This formula results from a study by the Passive House Platform and the Catholic University of Louvain and is intended to reflect the good compactness of large buildings.
[3] See Info-sheet (data sheet) 2.2. La conception de l'éclairage artificiel dans les logements et les bureaux (2010); www.bruxellesenvironnement.be > Particuliers > Thèmes > Eco-construction > Nos info-fiches.

Nos Pilifs, a passive workshop at Neder-Over-Heembeek [011]: in the north of Brussels has been built for the Nos Pilifs farm a non-profit organization offering employment to partially handicapped persons. Inserted into the embankment and covered with green roofs, the project is designed to minimize its impact on the environment. In the absence of a public sewer, the farm has also installed a system for the ecological treatment of part of its waste water by lagooning (J. Meganck, architect).

Renovation of listed buildings on the Boulevard de l'Impéra-trice [006]: the Royal Commis-sion for Monuments and Sites issues an opinion on any renovation project, which may or may not be binding. This applies, at least in part, to the transformations at Telex (Crepain Binst Architecture).

OFFICES AND ENERGY

The various Batex office projects have on average a net heating need of 24.7kWh/m² per year, falling to 15.4 kWh/m² for new constructions; in renovated buildings it rises to 41.7 kWh/m² (the cooling consumption of the MABRU project [069] is not included here).

Together, the Batex offices and shops annually save more than 1 250 000 litres of oil. Considering only the heating savings, the current rise in energy costs and the price of 0.90 €/l, the Batex subsidies represent less than 6 years of operation.

NET HEATING REQUIREMENT 2007-2011 RENOVATION OF OFFICES

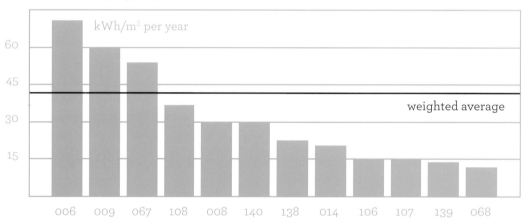

kWh/m² per year

weighted average

006 009 067 108 008 140 138 014 106 107 139 068

NET HEATING REQUIREMENT 2007-2011 CONSTRUCTION OF OFFICES

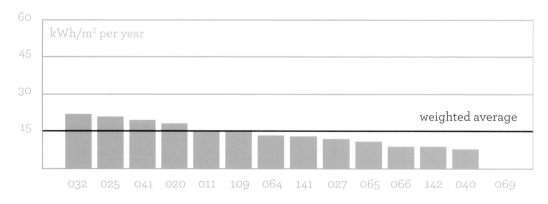

kWh/m² per year

weighted average

032 025 041 020 011 109 064 141 027 065 066 142 040 069

Aéropolis [040], a first office building delivered in 2010, has been followed by Marly office [065] and the MD2E site [066] in Forest, which will house an antenna for Actiris (the Brussels job seekers' office) and a series of services for job seekers, including a nursery. At Uccle, the municipal administration is building passive offices in a "hollow tooth" in Rue Beeckman [064]. Another small office project is the premises for the Gardens Department of the municipality of Evere in the Rue de l'Arbre Unique [109].

Passive offices on Quai Léon Monnoyer [141]: the external car park will be protected by the largest PV roof in Brussels, enabling the 4 000 m² of offices to move towards zero energy. All rain and waste water will be processed on site (Architectes Associés).

[TESTIMONY]
IN SEARCH
OF ECONOMIC OPTIMIZATION
THE RUE MONTOYER [107]
RENOVATION

What distinguishes a building that is truly made to last from another not designed to this requirement? With this office renovation project spotlighted by Batex in 2009, we already have the beginning of an answer...

"That very high energy performance buildings are very economic in the long run, I am convinced. When it comes to long-term operating, maintenance and replacement costs, I am more sceptical as regards the large amount of electronic and domotic equipment being used. We simlply do not yet know how this will perform in the long term...."

[1] The Befimmo portfolio totals two billion euros and some 850 000 m² of offices.
[2] Greenwashing is a mendacious form of discourse attributing allegedly green qualities to objects that do not actually present them. We also talk about eco-hypocrisy.

There are signs that do not lie. Where a developer would normally evoke with pride his "real estate portfolio", Rikkert Leeman, Chief Technical Officer at Befimmo[1], speaks of portfolio, values, investment, long-term investment... The references and guarantees he highlights in order to convince his "clients" are indicative of the times: ISO 14001 (environmental management system), ISA (International Sustainability Alliance), BREEAM ("BRE Environmental Assessment Method"), Batex... A financier in line with his times, we might say.

But when asked about greenwashing[2], he replies: "Our approach is not a marketing one. Our company is very discreet when you consider the size of its portfolio. We communicate little. What matters to us is the value of our portfolio. If we have been working consistently since 2006 on a sustainable development approach for all our buildings, it is precisely because it adds in the long term to the value of our business. We see an evolution of mentalities, that of the legislative framework also, all we are doing is anticipating. We really want to be among the 'front runners', in order to gain a competitive advantage over our competitors who stick strictly to what is required by regulations, without attempting to go beyond. This is not simply a question of packaging."

Demo version 2011 (end of construction), this office building in central Brussels, built in 1958, taken over in 2006 and completely revamped to last: undressing down to the skeleton, new skin, high performance glazing, condensation heating, free cooling, HVAC, solar protection, energy recovery elevator, bike storage with changing rooms and showers, 200 m² of photovoltaic panels, rainwater recovery tank (5 000 l)...

But no question of seeking performance for performance's sake. We could have gone for the passive standard liability, but we stayed just outside it (17 kWh/m² per year): "If we strive to always remain consistent with our sustainable development strategy, what guides us above all is the notion of cost effectiveness. We considered the economic optimum for this project to lie at E59/E60. The additional cost to reach passive building criteria proved excessive: in the case of this building we arrive at additional cost of around 9.5%, with a payback period of less than 10 years, which is reasonable."

And reason sometimes requires a certain caution that can act as a brake on innovation: "It is true that in terms of materials, the economic optimum means for us an analysis of the life cycle. It helps us make the right trade-off between financial investment, life expectation and sustainable development. This makes us very cautious in terms of innovation: while we can and must be innovative in terms of design and execution, we will probably think that much longer and harder when it comes to new materials..."

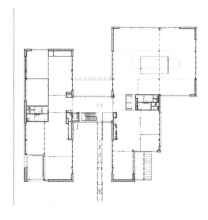

[BATEX 065 – MARLY] [1]

FBZ-FSE Electriciens | Avenue du Marly, at 1120 Neder-Over-Heembeek | FDZ-FSE | A2M sprl | Cenergie

COMMERCIAL, PASSIVE AND UNASHAMED

Three electricians' organizations, the Fonds de Sécurité d'Existence du secteur des électriciens (FSE Electriciens), Formelec and Tecnolec have opted to share headquarters in a newly-constructed building incorporating the best of energy-saving technologies.

Consultants DTZ guided them to the passive standard, especially for financial reasons[2] and Cenergie energy consultancy helped select architects A2M[3]. The building was delivered in November 2011.

GOING TOWARD THE LIGHT

Installed into a slope, like a signal at the entrance to the industrial estate, the project reserves the ground floor for the public part of its programme: large glazed front, training and meeting rooms, canteen, storage workshop and technical premises against the slope. Upstairs are the large landscaped offices open in all directions, with additional natural light provided by a large shed (also used for night ventilation).

BEYOND COMPACTNESS

The architects have designed a building that is passive, high performance and cost-efficient without making it into a compact cube. Marly multiplies overhangs and hollowing effects to form an H and thus benefit from the maximum possible amount of natural light and cross ventilation. In so doing, it loses compactness – and therefore needs to insulate a little more – but gains in economies of lighting. Electricity consumption is further reduced by 318 m² of photovoltaic panels.

A COMPOSITE STEEL/CONCRETE STRUCTURE

The bioclimatic requirements of a commercial building have led Marly to a solid structure – for its inertia – but not too much, to avoid adding too much weight to the overhangs. The structure is metallic (columns and beams) with concrete filling, with concrete slab floors and masonry walls. These are covered with 30 cm of coated graphite polystyrene. The terra cotta cladding is insulated with 28 cm of glass wool. The thermal bridges in the structure and the thousands of anchors for the cladding are limited by a thermal break detail and integrated into the overall calculation. Net heating need is reduced to 11 kWh/m² per year.

HYBRID VENTILATION

The risk of overheating is limited here by an underground heat exchanger that cools the air in summer (while preheating it in winter), and by night cooling. The system is hybrid: natural ventilation for most of the time, but a propeller fan helps extraction when the natural draft is insufficient. In normal mode, the windows open and close depending on needs and weather via a building management system (BMS). The regulation uses CO_2 sensors in the intermittently occupied parts of the building and occupancy sensors in offices. Consumption displays are integrated into the BMS.

[1] Read the report in be.passive 09, October 2011, p. 27 ff.
[2] See the "Value for Money" feature article in be.passive 09, October 2011.
[3] www.a2m.be

Passive offices and nursery at Rue de la Station [066]: to objectivize their eco-design choices, the architects of the MD2E offices used software that analyses the parameters of embodied energy, greenhouse gas emissions and consumption of water and other natural resources, along with renovation and recycling capacities. These parameters are aggregated in a 'score' that reflects the overall impact of the material (A2M architectes).

04/ NEW COMMERCIAL PASSIVE PROJECTS

Soon, the architects of Aéropolis II [040] will be extending the exercise with the Quai Léon Monnoyer project [141]: here the concrete structure will be made lighter and the envelope will be entirely in wooden caissons, into which the triple-glazed windows will be incorporated.

The Rue Belliard [142] project will be the largest passive promotional offices operation ever, with a building deemed obsolete destroyed to make way for a building with 14 levels. The project creates a large green public area to combat the "canyon" effect that characterizes the Rue Belliard. This area will communicate visually through a large glazed lobby with an enclosed garden. The Belliard project is clearly inspired by the Master Plan[1] of the nearby Rue de la Loi, which governs the densification of the European district and the redevelopment of the public space. The project by the winning architect Christian de Portzamparc provides for the erection of three tower blocks... that will be passive. Indeed, research[2] conducted to date shows passive building to be technically sound and financially viable for tall buildings. Perhaps these towers will be Batex winners one day?

[1] The Master Plan sets out a strategic vision for the development of zones of regional interest; http://urbanisme.irisnet.be
[2] Build Green seminar, *Les tours passives à Bruxelles : vers une faisabilité technique et économique ?*, 7.02.2012.

Passive offices on Avenue Britsiers [040]: an atrium has been built, running the whole height of the falsely compact Aéropolis II building, to bring in more natural light and facilitate intensive ventilation in summer (Architectes Associés).

Aéropolis II [040] (Architectes Associés).

At Uccle, the municipal administration is building passive offices in a "hollow tooth" in the Rue Beeckman [064]. The Municipality of Uccle entrusted this pilot project to its own architecture department which, in addition to the passive standard liability, also worked on the aspects of sustainable materials and optimization of natural light (D. Tramontana & A. De Decker).

Office renovation on Rue Vanpé [014]: when it comes to ventilation, we note the breakthrough of ventilation with heat recovery, even in delicate renovation operations (A2M architectes).

05/ AND THE TECHNICAL INSTALLATIONS?

The ambition to be "zero air conditioning" results in the absence of a cooling system. Engineer Piotr Kowalski[1] believes that to make the concept more robust, it is important to consider the possibility of extreme uses (e.g. 24/7 use of a building) and check that passive strategies such as night ventilation can function correctly.

Venting systems must be flexible to ensure adequate air flow in all circumstances: variable surface areas (with moving partition walls), variable population densities (and with fluctuating internal loads). This implies a certain oversizing and fine-tuned control systems.

In heating, the winter of 2011-2012 – with temperatures well below the dimensioning temperature – raises the question of it would not be better to redefine heating power from heating relaunch needs. The risk, of course, would give more flexibility to the user, even at the cost of increased consumption. For engineer Alain Bossaer[2], "Certain comfort requirements (e.g. higher ventilation rates and individual regulation of installations) raise some eyebrows in passive circles for conflicting with energy conservation. We must therefore seek a new balance in the passive concept. The standard becomes adult!"

THE EMERGENCE OF MICRO-CHP SYSTEMS

The first micro CHP (combined heat and power) or "co-generation" systems have made their appearance in Batex. These serve to produce both heat and electricity. Using gas, they permit energy savings of 15 to 20% compared with separate production. To further reduce CO_2 emissions, they can use a renewable fuel, such as rapeseed oil or pellets.

GEOTHERMAL ENERGY

Several office projects are implementing the concept of activated (concrete) slabs, in which water circulates at temperatures of 17 to 25 °C, depending on the season. The energy is collected by drilling into deep soil, where the temperature remains relatively stable over the year, and concentrated by a potentially reversible heat pump. The needs for heating and cooling need to be balanced on an annual basis, so as not to deplete the energy source.

A "Canadian well" underground heat exchanger is an "almost" passive form of geothermal system. It uses heat from the ground to heat the ventilation air in winter and, conversely, cool it in summer. It has been implemented in some twenty Batex projects. In an urban context, this type of ground heat exchanger is not always desirable since it demands both land and access for earthmoving machinery. The technology remains subject to certain hazards (such as land subsidence) and the difficulty of cleaning the pipes to maintain their sanitary quality. In an interesting urban variation, a ventilated cavity is used as a geothermal heat exchanger at Rue de la Cible [015]. To avoid these disadvantages and lack of space on the site, an underground head exchanger using glycolated water was introduced in Rue Wauters [017]. It is the water (not the air itself) that flows through the soil to recover heat in winter and cooling in summer and send it to the hygienic air.

ADIABATIC COOLING

To ensure summer comfort, air can be cooled by simply spraying water droplets on the outgoing air flow[3]. No energy input or microbiological control is necessary. The system consumes large quantities of water in summer, which can be partially recovered from the roof and filtered.

[1] See be.passive 04, June 2010, p. 38.
[2] See be.passive 07, April 2011, p. 48.
[3] See the exemplary buildings information sheets [066], [112] and [137].

Passive office renovation on Rue Nys [009]: these passive offices result from the conversion of a former 650 m² biology laboratory. The cubic volume of the storey has been wrapped with 24 cm of insulation, with a finishing coating. The ground floor is occupied by three low-energy homes (Architects Office Lahon & Partners).

Office renovation on Rue Vanpé [014]: the renovation of the Forest CPAS/OMCW offices has made it possible to reopen an attractive building that has stood empty for a long time, by reducing its heating need from 200 to 21 kWh/m²/year (A2M architectes).

Renovation and raising of a building on Rue de la Loi [068]: the Credibe building has been renovated to the very low energy standard, with the work phased to enable the occupants to remain on site. One principle has been to preserve as much as possible of the existing building (Synergy international).

TAKING RISKS?

The designer of the renovation in Rue Vanpé [014] chose to cut the floor to eliminate thermal bridges. This is a drastic measure with important consequences in terms of structure (you need to introduce new foundations and transfer loads) and the budget. For stability engineer Benoît Meersseman[1], this is more by way of experiment than setting an example, and he calls for caution: "if in new construction we are able to master all the challenges and can develop a form of exemplarity and replicability, I'm sure we are not there yet in renovation, nor am I sure that we will ever get there! We need to avoid creating unfortunate reflexes whereby in order to reduce a thermal bridge and obtain grant money, one takes decisions that are structurally rash…"

06/ BATEX OFFICES UNDER RENOVATION

The Brussels office market pushes operators to build new and abandon the old. This brings problems of demolition waste and pollution. Many offices are renovated into housing, but few… into offices.

Renovation of offices which are judged – at times with no objective criterion – as unsuitable is a real political message.

Located in the city centre and well served by public transport, Telex [006] is restoring a heritage jewel of the postwar period. The project reduces the heating need to 71 kWh/m² per year. A photovoltaic system produces 6 000 kWh per year.

The renovation of the municipality of Forest CPAS/OMCW offices in Rue Vanpé [014] in the Abbey of Forest protection zone has made it possible to reopen an endearing building that had stood empty for a long time, reducing the heating need from 200 to 21 kWh/m² per year.

Other projects also involve the roofs of buildings, on the occasion of an upward extension, like at Loi 42 [068] and Science-Montoyer [107]. When the "hat" is well-placed on the existing building, it significantly improves overall performance because a lot of heat in a building is lost through the roof. The offices at Rue Nys [009] convert a 650 m² former biology laboratory by wrapping its cubic volume in 24 cm of insulation, finished with a liquid coating. The system is naturally cooled in summer thanks to a strategy of night cooling linked to a temperature (and CO_2) control system.

[1] See his interview in be.passive 04, June 2010, p. 48.

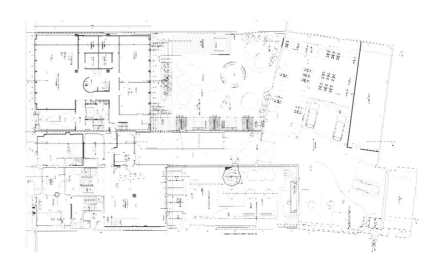

[BATEX 067 – RENOVATION MUNDO-B][1]

Rue d'Edimbourg 18-26 at 1050 Ixelles | Brussels Sustainable House (Mundo-B) | AAA Architectures | Ecorce

BRAVE OLD MUNDO

The Sustainable Development House – Mundo-B for short – brings together several associations in a central neighbourhood of Ixelles, providing them with 250 work stations, a cafeteria and a documentation centre in a building renovated by the Atelier d'Architecture A+A+A.

Commissioned by Ethical Property, the operation delivered in 2009 two 1950s buildings combined into one, reducing their net heating need from 138 to 52 kWh/m² per year with an n50 airtightness of 2 vol/h.

TARGETED, PRAGMATIC INTERVENTIONS

The project was intended to be ecological and pragmatic: to find a suitable abandoned office building, save and reuse what could be, reduce costs and amortize the additional costs through energy savings. The total cost of renovation amounted to € 811/m², of which 233 specifically for sustainability aspects. Grants included, the payback period is 7 years.

This result was achieved by insulating existing walls with standard thicknesses and raising one of the two buildings with an additional storey built in wood to the passive standard. The architects have given priority to the use of environmentally friendly materials in hemp wool, wood fibre, cellulose flocking for insulation, linoleum for floors, pigment paints, FSC certified wood, heat treated wood, a pellet boiler, etc.

Two ventilation systems complement each other, the first for the offices and the second for the meeting rooms. 100 m² of photovoltaic panels meet 7-8% of electricity needs and rainwater collected in a renovated cistern covers 25% of needs.

RAISING OCCUPANT AWARENESS

Raising occupant awareness of actual consumption forms the basis for any energy efficiency strategy. "The use of the place should lead everyone to feel responsible for the effect of their daily actions on the environment. In heating, for example, we chose not to impose anything: everyone can choose their own temperature and open their windows as they want. This means that we have a major job of communication ahead of us to explain the lifestyle that accompanies this type of building", says Frédéric Ancion[2], who posts consumption figures in the lobby and coordinates the spaces shared by tenants.

REPLICABILITY

With this experience under their belt, Frédéric Ancion and his team repeated the experience in Namur with N-Mundo, a renovation which goes as far as passive building and was delivered in 2010[3]. Other projects are under study. It is clear that many comparable buildings could draw inspiration from it and find a second life. Mundo-B has meanwhile received the Brussels Environment "Eco-dynamic undertaking" label.

[1] More on www.mundo-b.org
[2] See be.passive 05, September 2010, p. 23.
[3] Read the report in be.passive 04, June 2010, p. 59.

Sébastien Cruyt,
architect

[TESTIMONY]

THE CITY AT YOUR FEET, BETWEEN PLEASURE AND CONSTRAINTS RUE DE LA LOI 42 [068]

The office building dates from the thirties. A renovation was needed. With a client who is an economist and very committed to sustainability and a prime contractor who is at once visionary, ingenious and obstinate, it gives a result that is exemplary in many ways, in a European neighbourhood which is teeming with life during the daytime before turning at night into a languid urban desert.

"The initial reflex for any contractor would have been to demolish everything and start again from scratch. The idea of, instead, preserving as much as possible of what exists finally proved totally realistic in terms of the sought-after performance."

Rue de la Loi 42, 3 pm. The great motor cavalcade plunges into the city between office buildings, erected on both sides of the five traffic lanes. As you approach the inner ring, you look up. Up there, on top of five floors, large, dark cubes pile up. Like the nest of some bird, one might think. These luxury apartments are the only visible part of a development that is coming to an end after many long months of work. They were prefabricated, drawing their inspiration from the requirements of the passive standard, then raised and secured forty metres aloft by imposing cranes mounted on the garden side of the buildings.

The lower part of the project is an office complex dating from the thirties in two wings on either side of an inner courtyard. Here the renovation has been in-depth though almost imperceptible from the outside, despite being heightened with metal cladding. With an eco-focused objective: to preserve as much as possible of the existing building, recovering what deserves to be recovered and limiting the production of waste, to dramatically improve energy performance, without air conditioning and… allow the partial continuation of the company's activities (Credibe, the former OCCH) throughout the work, a demand that at times threatened to blow the planning to pieces. Only one candidate finally agreed to meet the challenge – too large for a small business, too complex for a large one – in agreement with the project owner, the very mediatic economist Eric De Keuleneer. And Sebastien Cruyt (Synergy International) openly admits that without his

If the particularly demanding repair of the old building proved exemplary in many ways – both for the complexity of the technical difficulties and for the originality of the solutions developed and patience devoted to their implementation – it is of course the placing on the top of the building of passive homes, made of prefabricated metal modules, a variant not originally foreseen in the specifications, which draws people's attention. First because it is a wager on housing in a neighbourhood of the capital where "multifunctionality" is most lacking, and as such contributes to an increasingly desired densification of housing.

Then because it was able to play on the technical difficulties of building passive housing in the centre of town, at a place where a traditional building site would probably have posed insurmountable problems. A formula that Cruyt does not deny, even if, on reflection, an approach based on walls rather than volumes would have seemed to him better suited to the constraints specific to passive housing.

Be that as it may, the final effect is surprising, in terms of the refound comfort of the offices, the quality of sound insulation and the luminosity of the new homes perched above the city.

Passive housing and commercial area on the Place des Etangs Noirs [132]: Batex projects include several commercial areas which are integrated into mixed projects. With ten passive housing units and a commercial area that can be modulated for a variety of activities, the architects have sought to make the building as compact and well-oriented as possible. In a desire for social integration, all apartments are accessible to disabled people (R²D² architecture).

Renovation of a carpentry workshop on Rue Faes [008]: the project consists of effectively insulating the building and installing a set of solar heating and photovoltaic panels (2 x 18 m²). Everything is thought out in terms of short loops: less travel (housing on site), use of carpentry waste (for heating) and rainwater (via a 5 m³ tank). A factory chimney has been converted into a vertical garden (Modelmo Marc Opdebeek architect).

Renovation of a listed industrial building on Rue Dieudonné Lefèvre [139]: built in 1925, this former factory building used to produce a wine aperitif named "Byrrh". The Brussels CPAS/OCMW will be renovating this listed industrial building into a centre for urban economic activities. The walls of the building will be insulated. The heated spaces will be ventilated by a double flow system with heat recovery (JZH & Partners/Ozon architecture/N. Créplet).

07/ ONE-OFF OBJECTS

Two complex operations are intended to install programmes which are themselves complex: the renovation of the Byrrh site [139] will provide a cluster of urban activities, including work areas for Brussels entrepreneurs and shared amenities (cafeteria and crèche), while the Alchimiste building [108] was intended to be renovated into a business centre, but the project is currently stalled.

This type of intervention seeks to preserve the identity of the buildings by insulating them from the inside, enabling Byrrh to achieve a net heating need of between 14 and 27 kWh/m² per year. The walls have been carefully designed to avoid any risk of humidity and deterioration.

Batex projects include several commercial spaces which are part of mixed projects. The largest is indisputably the Caméléon sales warehouse [025].

Three projects develop small industrial activities: installing a joiner's shop and dwelling in a former industrial building in Rue Faes [008], the passive workshop built for the Nos Pilifs farm association [011] and the MABRU early morning market [069], which is building, not a heated building, but huge "brick-and-concrete" fridges, with the aim of optimizing the quality of their insulation (18 cm) and inertia.

Passive homes on Rue Wauters [017]: "Living in a home where there are no cold areas is a real luxury! The sensations of life also change. In winter, for example, one no longer says 'I'm cold', huddling up close to a radiator or a wood fire. In passive housing, the temperature is uniform, regular and pleasant throughout the house. There is no one room at 20°C and the other at 12°C. One can be in T-shirt or sweater in the same way everywhere." Inès Camacho, architect and inhabitant

SUSTAINABLE
ARCHITECTURES

At the heart of a large metropolitan area, the Brussels-Capital Region, with its 19 municipalities and nearly 1.1 million inhabitants, is a powerful economic machine. With 10% of the country's population, it produces 19% of the national GDP. Each day, one employee in two and one school student out of seven arrives in Brussels from one of the other regions.

Passive social housing on Rue Loossens [016]: "as a public service housing company, we are seeking to improve our service to our tenants and to offer them comfortable homes with major energy savings", the Foyer Jettois explained in 2009 (A2M architectes).

But Brussels is the living space for its inhabitants. Behind its economic success, the Region needs to combat the degradation and impoverishment of its territory[1], where the average income is just 82%[2] of the national average. The Region is seeing a gradual polarization of its population, with high unemployment, while rents and real estate prices continue to surge…

These socio-economic disparities translate into a high degree of inequality in housing, health and environmental quality. Fuel poverty is having social impacts that we are just beginning to measure. Life expectancy is six years shorter or longer depending on whether one lives in Saint-Josse-ten-Node or Woluwe-Saint-Pierre[3]. Every year urban stress leads one Brussels inhabitant in ten to leave the region… to be replaced by a less well-off newcomer[4].

In short, Brussels is a city of paradoxes: it cannot accommodate "all the misery of the world" with the attendant insecurity, but nor can it accommodate "all the riches of the world", which generates a spatially and economically unsustainable segregation. This city that places everyone in competition with each other will be fully sustainable only to the extent that it finds a way out of this contradiction.

Contemporary metropolises like Brussels need to learn to function differently. They face environmental challenges, such as reducing their greenhouse gas emissions and searching for energy alternatives to cheap oil, that raise intimate social and economic questions. Faced with this, Brussels is committed to improving the quality of life of its residents and ensuring their equal access to a quality environment. In 2004, Brussels-Capital initiated a vast effort of restructuring its ambitions and its energy policies. Noting that the sector was in urgent need of support, it laid the foundations of its approach to sustainable construction.

This collective effort has borne much fruit: first of all, professionals today know much better what they are talking about. "Batex has allowed us to do a lot of experimenting, both in engineering offices and on construction sites, and it is pretty exciting now to have the feedback that was not there 4 or 5 years ago. Everyone understands each other better, and we also understand better what we are saying because everyone has acquired a more concrete knowledge of things", reports architect Olivier Mathieu. The concepts of energy need and design logic and the need to give priority to simple solutions, all these are beginning to enter people's consciousnesses, and Brussels is moving towards sustainable buildings that are no longer the technology "Christmas trees" of the first decade of the millennium.

[1] *Rapport sur l'état de la pauvreté 2011*, Observatoire de la Santé et du Social de Bruxelles-Capitale, www.observatbru.be
[2] Compared with 90% in 2000: Wealth Index Indicator, www.monitoringdesquartiers.irisnet.be, *Dossier du baromètre conjoncturel n° 12: 20 ans d'évolutions socio-économiques bruxelloises* (2009).
[3] For men, health indicators taken from www.monitoringdesquartiers.irisnet.be
[4] Mini-Bru 2012, Institut bruxellois de Statistiques et d'Analyse, edition 2011.

Passive school, offices and housing on Rue Simons [137]: the project is for the construction of 51 units in the context of the growing demand for housing in Brussels. To complete the offering, offices for the ONE-Kind & Gezin (government child welfare agency) are integrated into the building to form a coherent whole (A2M architectes).

Passive school on Rue de la Rosée [154]: the project consists of the building of an extension for the Arts and Crafts Institute (IAM) including body-work and mechanical works-hops, classrooms, dining hall and an infrastructure for the advanced technologies centre (CTA). The passive standard is respected and, by further reducing its energy dependence, the project comes close to zero carbon (MDW architectes).

01/ WHERE DO THE BATEX SUBSIDIES GO?

Which Brussels municipalities benefit from Batex subsidies? Each municipality has its own characteristics and special needs. A "poor" municipality – where for example the wealth index[1] in 2009 was only 52% of the national average wealth will have different needs and will offer different opportunities than the wealthiest municipality with an index of 115%.

Taking into account the population and average income in each municipality, we see that Batex is of particular interest to project leaders in municipalities with low incomes/wealth indices and with correlatively the youngest populations. Batex seems to be better known and enjoy greater public policy support here than in wealthier municipalities with older populations.

A particular reason for this is that several Batex operations are related to Sustainable Neighbourhood Contracts and other urban programmes. The municipality of Brussels-City, for example, has 188 Batex-labelled dwellings in its 1000 Homes plan.

It is Brussels-City (including Laeken, Haren, and Neder-Over-Heembeek) that seems most "committed", with an index 2.7 times higher than the regional average. Saint-Josse-ten-Node, Forest, Schaerbeek, Molenbeek-Saint-Jean and Anderlecht follow close behind. The other municipalities are less dynamic than the regional average.

Are Batex projects the Trojan horse of gentrification[2]? It is true that they are concentrated in low-income municipalities with economically at-risk populations. Yet this hidden gentrification does not appear to be the case, given the preponderance of public housing and other buildings (two Batex dwellings out of three are public). The creation or renovation of social housing is one way to fight price pressure and the gentrification effect. On the other hand, the average size of the houses (175 m²) and apartments (106 m²) remains in the basic housing category. The Batex

sustainable construction goals appear to have been recognized and incorporated in the road-maps of social players to strengthen their presence and activity in those parts of the Region where the housing stock and collective infrastructures no longer meet the current demands of households.

It's harder to answer this question for private and BRDA projects: the future of Midi-Suède [034] and Espoir [060] will tell us in 10 years: will these properties be sold on by their owners? Do we need another form of property ownership to create speculation-free areas? How do we exercise a greater influence on the private sector, which represents over 90% of supply?

[1] www.monitoringdesquartiers.irisnet.be/maps/revenus/revenus-fiscaux/indice-de-richesse/0/2009/
[2] Gentrification is a socioeconomic phenomenon that can accompany neighbourhood renewal: the building work improves the housing stock, raising rents, pushing out small businesses and excluding at-risk populations in favour of wealthier households. To avoid this, a supply of public housing and support for businesses need to be put in place.

02/ AND ENERGY?

Already in 2007, the first call marked the distance that existed then between certain winning projects: from the private Albatross development [026] to the Aéropolis offices [040] or the first zero energy passive housing[1] in Rue Loossens [016], we move from 39 to 8 or even 0 kWh/m²!

Since 2008, all new housing and office projects have adopted the passive standard, together with 13 renovation projects.

In renovation the same big span is palpable – from 15 to 71 kWh/m², but this depends on the condition of the original buildings. The margin narrows from one Batex to the next, while the range of renovated buildings on the contrary continues to grow: in 2011, the renovation of the Laeken swimming pool [145] brought consumption down from almost 500 kWh/m² to 58!

In terms of energy efficiency, the results are impressive, both for new construction and for renovation. The energy savings achieved in both new construction (compared to the current PEB requirement) and renovation (compared to the average energy needs of the sector) are estimated at an annual gain of more than 3 385 000 litres of oil or 2 900 tonnes[2] year after year. The production of renewable energy adds the equivalent of 155 000 litres of oil savings.

The individual housing sector achieves the highest energy saving per m², but at a higher cost. Grants are amortized, in energy savings alone and taking into account the current rise in energy costs, in less than 7 years. For other sectors, the pay-back period is less than 6 years. In terms of specific heating need in new and renovated buildings, studies show the following results:

AVERAGE NET HEATING NEED (KWH/M² PER YEAR)	NEW	RENOVATION
single dwelling	16.8	27.2
collective housing	14.5	23.4
amenities	18.4	35.4
offices, shops, workshops	15.4	41.6

In residential housing, the heating needs of renovated buildings are reduced by a factor of more than 5 times from the average of 150 kWh/m² for existing buildings to 23 to 27 kWh/m² after renovation! Overall, 75% of new Batex homes reach the passive standard, and their proportion has risen from 39% in 2007 to 93% in 2011. For amenities and offices the net heating need (renovation) is still a little higher, given the wider range of activities and their specific needs.

All these results also depend on users' behaviour: how do they occupy the building? Architect Evert Crols: "We are curious to see how the passive buildings will be experienced by their occupants. We believe it is imperative to accompany occupiers, so as to avoid any unpleasant surprises", concern shared by many clients, as we saw with the homes in the L'Espoir project [060].

The results also depend on the readiness of building companies and architects to adopt new practices – and also on rapidly changing requirements. Certain ways of applying the passive standard have evolved over time: with the passive character first of all imposed on the building as a whole and then to each dwelling unit separately. Some engineering offices need closer supervision with certain technical acts such as the blower door test…

With a quarter of the floor space delivered and another quarter under construction right now, it is clear that this level of energy efficiency is available to many building owners who take a proactive approach. "We now need to widely disseminate the accumulated experience and make it available to the market to stabilize the advances made in Brussels" concludes engineer Bram De Meester.

CATEGORIES	m²	SUBSIDY (€)	€/m²	SAVINGS (l)	l/m²	PAY-BACK PERIOD
single dwelling	9 465	941 827	100	101 457	10.7	< 7 years
collective housing	101 661	7 443 842	73	964 967	9.5	< 6 years
amenities	111 978	7 710 827	69	1 057 111	9.4	< 6 years
offices, shops, workshops	148 820	7 154 674	51	1 261 698	8.5	< 6 years
total		**23 251 171**	**63**	**3 385 232**	**9.1**	**< 6 years**

[1] Only the house in Rue Baron Vandernoot [125] is holding out…
[2] One tonne of oil equivalent (toe) is 11 600 kWh.

Passive housing on Avenue Dubrucq [018]: after decontamination of the land, eight passive social housing units have been built, along with a nursery, a multi-purpose room for the neighbourhood and logistics premises for the management of a new public park (B architecten).

Renovation on Avenue Besme [054]: this Art Deco project achieves good energy performance despite the difficulty of preserving the architectural heritage (48 kWh/m²/year heating requirement) (A-Cube architecture).

03/ AND HERITAGE BUILDINGS?

The question takes a very different form when the building is, by government decision, protected in whole or in part and to varying degrees: listing, protection zones, safeguard lists, etc.

The Royal Commission for Monuments and Sites then issues an opinion on any renovation project, which can be binding or not. This is the case, in whole or in part, for the conversion work at Télex [006], Rue Vanpé[1] [014], the Byrrh warehouse[139], the Chaussée de Forest home[2] [046], the homes and offices in Avenue Besme [054], Rue du Tilleul [057], Avenue Ducpétiaux [077], Rue du Moulin [088] and Rue de Montenegro [119].

With already-built architecture, particularly heritage sites, energy comes a long way down the list in terms of concerns. With its implications in terms of atmosphere and varied forms of comfort (or discomfort), the building itself takes precedence over the simple question of heating. Moreover, older forms of architecture have positive qualities (of inertia, etc.) that can be put to good advantage, if we accept that their "sustainable" uses translate into a comfort level that will never be that of a new building.

Clearly, preservation of heritage buildings reduces architects' room for manoeuvre and limits the energy savings, especially when the insulation needs to be discreet. Checking on a case by case basis, the qualitative leap after the building work is exemplary and does not call into question either the social choice to preserve the historical witnesses of our heritage, or that of improving their overall environmental efficiency.

The passive renovations witness to the personal involvement of owners in the renovation work and in environmental issues. They also show that the high construction quality involves a change in the relation of the inhabitant to his living framework: he can no longer be a mere consumer, but needs to become an architect and guardian. In the case of Rue des Archives [081], a third and simpler element came into play: with the Batex subsidies, it was cheaper to renovate to the passive standard than to the current PEB standard...

[1] See *be.passive* 08, June 2011, p. 67.
[2] See *be.passive* 07, April 2011, p. 67.

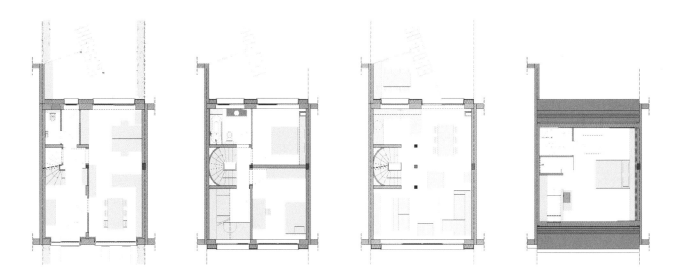

[BATEX 081 – PASSIVE RENOVATION IN THE RUE DES ARCHIVES][1]

Rue des Archives 28 at 1170 Watermael-Boitsfort | Nicodème Hélène and Tilman Raphaël | Nicodème Hélène and Tilman Raphaël

SUPER EXCITED

Even when one is an architect, embarking on a renovation remains a challenge, especially when it involves the family home. Especially that of a young couple. And particularly when the intended end result is a passive house.

"At our age we could not have put together the necessary sum" [for the purchase and renovation], say architects and owners Hélène Nicodème and Raphaël Tilman. "A helping hand from our parents allowed us to gradually put together the resources needed, given the Batex subsidy. The return on investment comes out to around ten years…" They have occupied the house since 2010.

INSULATING FROM THE OUTSIDE

It was possible to renovate the house mainly by insulating from the outside. This presents a significant advantage in a house where every square inch of floor space is counted. A coating placed on a 20 cm panel of graphite-added polystyrene gives today a more compact, mural appearance to the whole. Only the ground floor had, for urban planning reasons, to be insulated from the inside, creating a small number of thermal bridges to be reduced or eliminated. Obtaining good airtightness was more laborious, but a nice n50 value of 0.52 vol/h

rewards their efforts. The roof is made of composite beams and insulated with cellulose.

OPENING UP A NARROW SPACE

Initially, Raphael remembers, "we had the classic pattern of a 'bel-étage' house, with a completely closed L-shaped living room. We chose to break open all the load-bearing walls and replace them with posts. The space is now completely open to the stairwell." This is the main benefit of a passive building in terms of spatiality: no more need for thermal buffers since everything is heated in the same way, with small, cramped, old-fashioned rooms naturally combined into a much more generous, transparent and luminous living space. A result of which, in Helen's words, even the grandparents, the first occupants of the house, were "super excited!"

BEWARE OF PARTY WALLS

When the house next door was sold in winter, it ceased to be heated and the indoor climate

suffered. Things returned to normal only when new neighbours moved in and the heating system was restarted… A simple answer to this lack of foresight can be provided by oversizing the backup heating.

REPLICABILITY

The house in the Rue des Archives is a very common model in Brussels, and its conversion should also be relatively easy to reproduce. This is an important issue for all neighbourhoods in the "second circle" of suburbs (Evere, Woluwe-Saint-Lambert, Woluwe-Saint-Pierre, Auderghem, Watermael-Boitsfort, Uccle, Berchem-Sainte-Agathe and Ganshoren). Moreover, the house next door has just been renovated, drawing on the technical choices made by Hélène and Raphael… with an entirely different use of space: further proof that the objectives of sustainable construction do not encroach on freedom of design!

[1] Read the report in *be.passive* 06, January 2011, p. 69.

Hélène Nicodème
and Raphaël Tilman,
promoters, architects
and inhabitants

[TESTIMONY]

A "BEL ÉTAGE"
REGAINS ITS YOUTH
RUE DES ARCHIVES [081]

They have remodelled from top to bottom a modest house in a quiet area of Boitsfort.
With a desire which gnaws at today's young architects: anticipating upcoming
changes of urban society, in all its dimensions. And passing on to those around them
the lessons they have learned...

"In renovation, you discover a host of things as you go along. You need to remain creative and imaginative. In this sense our house became for us, as architects, a real laboratory."

This is a "bel étage" (living room on the first floor) house as they were built by the dozens in Brussels, in the sixties. Constructed in brick, in a very quiet street of Watermael-Boitsfort which includes several dozen such houses built terrace-fashion along the same lines, alongside the Brussels-Luxembourg railway line (and soon the future RER[1]) which passes in a cutting on the other side of the street.

Built economically in solid brick, terraced, continuous windows, a good one hundred fifty square metres of living space over four levels of about forty-eight square metres each, thin intermediate walls, central staircase, some rooms a bit small...

A familiar place for Hélène Nicodème who, as a child, often visited her grandmother in this family home on Wednesday afternoons or on weekends. She and her husband, Raphael Tilman, both architects, acquired it a few years ago to make it their home, and initially, also their offices.

The renovation needed to adapt the building to a more contemporary living style and living spaces, automatically meant, for these "professionals", a design dominated by the greatest possible energy sobriety. Initially they turned it into a low or very low energy building, then with the help of Call for Exemplary Buildings (2009) a real passive house (at the time there existed just one in Brussels!).

Which implies not only a very thorough insulation of the envelope (here on the outside for the upper floors and on the inside for the ground floor) and airtightness; an approach at the time still considered unrealistic for a renovation job. "At first they thought we were all crazy", Raphaël Tilman admits.

The first sketches saw the internal load-bearing walls disappear, replaced by supporting columns to give a wide open living space, with an open staircase. In the process, the garage disappeared to become the future office, with triple glazing to reduce the noise of the trains (which over time would prove to be very discreet, given the sunken situation of the tracks). The space under the roof was raised, in order to fit in an extra room, featuring a shower and a small discreet cupboard housing all the technical equipment: central heating, ventilation, etc.

But that was not the most spectacular element. The challenge for the young architects was the insulation, the hunt for "leaks" and ventilation. A patient task of tracking and covering all the "details", like the passage of electrical conduits and ventilation ducts, downpipes or difference in level with the neighbouring roofs, following the raising of the roof.

An insightful experience which they would like to share in the form of a "table d'hôte" on the ground floor, to explain to passing hosts their way of bringing the passive standard into the renovation of modest houses in Brussels...

[1] At this point, the tracks pass in a cutting parallel to the road. The projects include a covering this section of the track with a planted covering, with a park and allotments, linking Boitsfort railway station and the Forêt de Soignes.

House renovation, Rue de la Clinique [045]: besides the energy saving concept of the dwelling, the choice of bio-ecological materials and the good location in relation to public transport, the good indoor air quality is guaranteed by a system of double-flow ventilation with heat recovery (D. Dardenne, L. Collignon, architects).

IN THE WORDS OF AN ARCHITECT

"In our new offices, there are twelve months of perfect, constant, temperate climate! So much so that some customers prefer having the meetings on our premises..."

Architect Michel Henry [009]

"Living in a home where there are no cold areas is a true luxury! The sensations of life also change. In winter, for example, one no longer says 'I'm cold', huddling up to a radiator or a wood fire. In passive housing, the temperature is uniform, regular and pleasant throughout the house. There is no one room at 20°C and the other at 12°C. One can be in T-shirt or sweater in the same way everywhere."

Architect and resident Inès Camacho [017]

"When you do passive building under the Batex flag, this sets the standard very high: there are the technical performances, but there are also enormous expectations from users, who tolerate less discomfort than in existing buildings. People are waiting with a gun for designers if things go wrong."

Architect Pierre Somers

04/ AND COMFORT?

Measuring energy savings without evaluating the comfort of the inhabitants makes little sense. Brussels Environment has launched a survey of Batex householders.

The first results cover 27 units, or 8 houses and 19 apartments. 20 dwellings are new and 7 are renovations, 21 are passive, 4 are very low energy and 2 are low energy. 22 are owner occupied, 5 are rented.

Of course, for each project, we could compile a long list of micro-defects to be rectified: a vent to be adjusted, a coating to be corrected, etc. This is obviously not the place. All these hiccups will gradually be sorted out.

After the first wave of replies, it appears that temperatures are widely perceived as comfortable (neither too hot nor too cold), with a tendency for a fraction of the occupants to feel "hot" in the summer and sometimes too cold in winter. The satisfaction rate is 85% in summer and 77% in winter[1].

[1] It is never higher (?? Note that in such surveys it is never higher than 95%) (there is always a dissatisfaction rate of at least 5%), a score that conventional buildings very rarely obtain...

INTERIOR TEMPERATURE SUMMER

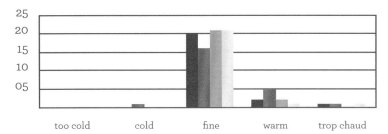

INTERIOR TEMPERATURE WINTER

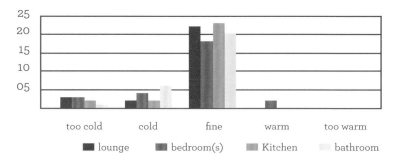

Renovating a listed house on Avenue Besme [054]: preserving and renovating the Art Deco frames by installing double glazing and placing joints to the right of the striking edges of the opening windows (A-Cube architecture).

Passive housing on Avenue Dubrucq [018]: the nursery nestled under the housing units is level with the adjacent public park and directly accessible from the street (B-architecten).

Renovation of listed offices in Boulevard de l'Impératrice [006]: the offices are cooled by chilled ceilings. After absorbing heat from the rooms needing to be cooled, the water circulating through the chilled ceilings is used to preheat the fresh air (Crepain Binst Architecture).

The air humidity seems also widely perceived as comfortable (92%) in summer and winter (85%). Lighting and acoustic comfort, odour control, etc. seem very satisfactory, with satisfaction scores between 80 and 90%.

This does not prevent reference points from changing slightly: "The difference with a normal house? It's that here one is deceived by the comfort! We dress lightly and once outside, we realize that it is far too cool…" admit architects and inhabitants Hélène Nicodème and Raphaël Tilman [081].

AIR HUMIDITY SUMMER

AIR HUMIDITY WINTER

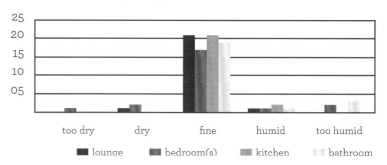

COMFORT

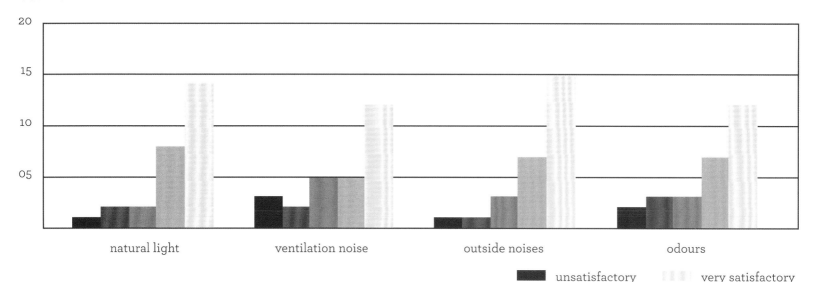

Renovation of offices on Rue Vanpé [014]: preserving the original façade, the architects chose to insulate the front from the inside. The old steel window frames have been preserved in the façade and new high-performance frames placed inside to ensure users' thermal and acoustic comfort (A2M architectes).

Renovation and heightening
of a building on Rue de la Loi
[068]: the building's central
location prevented the use
of traditional solutions, so the
heightening was done using
passive prefabricated
modules based on a light steel
structure and complemented
by a wood substructure
(Synergy International).
> *be.passive* 10, March 2012.

Renovation of offices on Rue Vanpé [014]: the Karsten pipe test, which defines the characteristics of moisture transfer through the wall (A2M architectes).

House renovation on Avenue du Diamant [033]: the renovation led to the existing walls being fully lined on the inside with an insulated wooden frame. Particular attention was also paid to controlling humidity transfers (Modelmo, M. Opdebeek, architect).

Rue Montagne Saint-Job [021]: new materials, TTI beams and integrated insulation (G. Bedoret, architect).

SUSTAINABLE CONSTRUCTION IN FIGURES

Overall, it should be noted that among the winning projects,
98% have reinforced insulation (from K30 to K15)
98% use a double-flow ventilation with heat recovery
85% use renewable energy: biomass, photovoltaic or thermal panels
87% have implemented passive cooling strategies
92% have renovated or installed a cistern or manage rainwater on their plot
84% use mostly eco-materials
88% have adopted a strategy to reduce and/or recycle building waste
83% have developed their project to promote non-motorized means of transport, such as cycling
67% have greened all or part of their roof
61% have adopted materials conducive to health and comfort
49% contribute to enhancing local biodiversity.

05/ AND SUSTAINABLE CONSTRUCTION?

The first results of the satisfaction survey of occupants carried out by Brussels Environment show that these strategies have a positive overall impact on daily life: if car travel does not appear to be affected by Batex, control of heating, electricity and water consumption seems to have improved, as has the relationship to the natural world.

For customer Benoît Ceysen: "In twenty years, technologies have consolidated tremendously and, unlike once upon a time with straw-earth technologies, one can today develop a very coherent building by carefully selecting and integrating the different possibilities." The health and environmental impact of "good" materials remains a subject of scientific research. Architects take training, peruse atlases, reference manuals, etc., but the numbers are very complex to validate and the impact of design choices difficult to assess.

Otherwise, technologies which were almost unknown yesterday are found today in almost all the winning projects. Alain Demol: "For the construction company this means new applications that have to be learned, and like any novelty be properly managed. Whether you place 10 or 30 cm of insulation makes little difference in terms of placing technique, but it can for some accessories…" Combined with a high efficiency, these materials and technologies still have to be monitored to check their durability over time,

resistance to humidity flows, temperature cycles, seasonal differences in rainfall and to wear and tear. "We need to help the building trades to evolve", says contractor Yvan Zoppé. "The person I most fear is the old bricklayer who says: 'I've always done it like that and it's never been a problem.' It's no good answering: "You've been wrong for the past forty years and should have done it otherwise.' But rather: 'We've just discovered that with this particular flick of the wrist it will be even better. And this flick of the wrist, only

Passive social housing on Rue du Libre Examen [090]: this forgotten corner is today being watched over by a building where the simple luxury of a little more space than "usual" makes you want to live there. Generous service areas are located on the ground floor… (Délices Architectes).

Passive housing on Rue du Pépin [062]: these units are faced with an attractive but poisonous copper skin. The architects compensated the choice of this ecologically negative metal with other ecologically positive construction items (Conix Architects).

you, with the experience you have, can do perfectly. We need you.' Who would not be delighted to hear that?"

However, experience shows that certain materials or systems do not keep all their promises. For Ecorce's consulting engineers, the airtightness of OSB panels is poor, as are the performance and maintenance of grey water recycling systems. In average public buildings, wood cladding must also meet fire resistance categories that call for chemical – and not necessarily ecological – treatment. Solutions like coatings on top of wood fibre are not accepted by control offices.

While the technologies of green roofs and rainwater distribution are now collective knowledge, putting the two together still raises questions: rainwater recovered downstream of a green roof is unclean and contains particles of matter. The Batex rules raise still other sustainable construction issues: what criteria should one apply in assessing the merits and demerits of a demolition? Do not certain energy aspects (mainly hunting down thermal bridging) compete with structural aspects? Cutting slabs or wood floors remains a risky operation and longevity of some solutions (such as frames with thermal breaks) is still unknown…

Batex designers have opened a debate which opposes two visions. The first is an "intuitive" vision based on well-being and on sustainability tied to certain natural materials like wood, hemp, etc. some of the qualities of which are emphasized by the NIBE reference framework. The second vision seeks to reduce the environmental footprint of the project while making it more sustainable both socially – making use of building companies' existing bricklaying, plastering and similar skills – and economically – with more affordable unit prices than wood construction permits.

LIFESTYLE

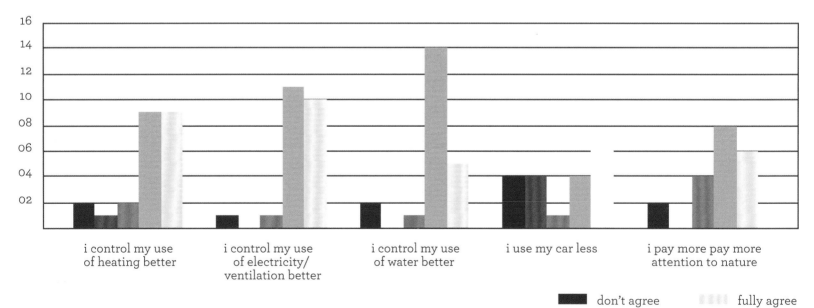

| | i control my use of heating better | i control my use of electricity/ ventilation better | i control my use of water better | i use my car less | i pay more pay more attention to nature |

don't agree   fully agree

THE EXPERTS SPEAK

For Alain Demol of building company DHERTE: "On a passive construction site, it is even more important for everyone to pay attention to the work of the others, especially so as not to degrade the airtightness and insulation, where special efforts are made. Communication and monitoring: An electrician or plumber who is not aware of what a passive building is can, in an hour or a day, wreck several months' work by other trades. So, we are continually monitoring, it's the only viable approach."

Architect Vincent Szpirer: "What makes the difference is not so much the difficulty of the passive standard, but rather the ability of a firm to manage its subcontractors or deal with the situation when one of them does not turn up."

06/ AND THE TECHNOLOGIES?

If the structural work of a sustainable project more or less resembles that of a traditional building, it is the emphasis given to insulation in general and to airtightness in particular that makes the difference. Placing insulation has become a profession in itself.

As has air sealing, which requires extreme care. Entrepreneur Christophe Cardinael: "We trained together, from senior managers to site foremen, including all subcontractors and all managers down to the site workmen. For us, success is possible only if everyone understands exactly what he is doing and why." The results are today checked on site by thermal imaging and blower door tests. New businesses have been created to meet these new needs.

THE HARD APPRENTICESHIP OF AIRTIGHTNESS

If there is one technical operation that scares companies, it is air sealing. It is a basically simple operation, but it requires care, and therefore time, and therefore costs money. Some architects are conscious of this, others not, and others too much so, imagining the task to be impossible. Same thing for building companies. According to Denis Lefébure, "there is a very important difference between contractors with experience in passive building (and therefore air sealing) and those who lack this experience. Without wishing to generalize, the former will address the question of airtightness before putting the spade in ground,

while the others will not bother until one month before the first blower door® test."

Contrary to what is still often reported, the airtightness is not something that can be resolved solely on site (read: under the responsibility of the building company). On the contrary, the entire design, from sketches to detail work, has a fundamental impact on the final result.

A great many details, as part of the frames for the blinds, letter boxes, doorbells, kitchen hoods, etc. need new solutions. The electrical system poses new problems, fortunately easy to solve if they are considered on time. Briefing notes[1] are published by Brussels Environment to meet the specific issues of stairwells, elevators, technical shafts, openings linked to special ventilation-related technologies. The same notes also list the conditions for airtightness testing, particularly for large buildings.

In many projects, airtightness tests need to be repeated before being conclusive; the cost is increasingly being picked up by the builders themselves. It does not, however, seem to be so

high for them to want to purchase the equipment and perform these tests themselves. "Our relationship with construction companies has changed, partly because of our Batex projects. I find that companies, even those that are not specially trained in passive building, frankly have done a very good job in picking up the gauntlet", concludes architect Sebastian Moreno-Vacca.

VENTILATION AND HEAT EXCHANGER

In terms of installations, we observe the breakthrough of mechanical ventilation with heat recovery. Of course, this appears imperative in the energy balance of buildings. Even if we would sometimes like to be without it, because it is paradoxical to break one's back to consume less heating... and then run fans! There also remains an archaic fear: that of suffocating in the event of

[1] Data sheets 1.1 and 1.2: Airtightness (2010); www.bruxellesenvironnement.be > Particuliers > Thèmes > Eco-construction > Nos info-fiches; see also CSTC-Contact n°33 (1.2012), *L'étanchéité à l'air des bâtiments : un défi majeur pour l'ensemble des corps de métier*, Centre Scientifique et Technique de la Construction, www.cstc.be > Publications > CSTC-Contact

Renovation and heightening of a building Rue de la Loi [068]: given the noise and pollution of cars on the Rue de la Loi, this mixed passive office and residential project provides intensive ventilation solely from openings on the rear façade, supported where necessary by mechanical ventilation (Synergy international).

a power blackout... It's worth reminding people here that all windows can be opened, even in passive housing. The interactions between new technologies – especially in terms of regulation – need to be refined: For client Hilde De Wandeler, "The hardest part of the adventure of our building was to understand the implications of each technology on the others."

The first results of the satisfaction survey, however, show that the ventilation is well appreciated by the occupants, with an overall score of 80% for both summer and winter:

The air quality is rated between 8.5 and 9/10 depending on the rooms. One person in five opens windows – summer and winter – while four out of five do not feel the need.

Even so, it is important that ventilation systems be kept clean, with best practice to prevent transmission of sounds, smells, etc. and giving occupants the ability to manage their own ventilation. Architect Pierre Blondel is concerned by the "lack of perspective that we have on passive building and on the coaching people need on moving into passive housing. What will become of the passive homes we are building today in 10 or 20 years?" A good reason to visit passive buildings constructed, as in Germany, since 1991.

REGULATION
Special care is needed in regulating both small and large buildings: the balance of heat and cold is "tense", the responsiveness of the building is slow, and the heating installations are underpowered by normal standards. Much of this is played out "in real time", provided that the parameters controlling supplementary heating or night cooling are adequate. For large buildings, "commissioning" is an essential step – which can take from one to two years – for optimizing the operation of the building[1]. Whichever way an individual lives, a passive building will always consume much less than a conventional building.

[1] See the "Fine Tuning" feature article, *be.passive* 07, April 2011, p. 42-49.

SUMMER VENTILATION
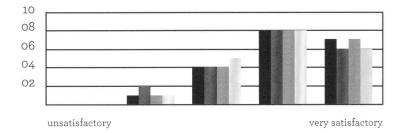

WINTER VENTILATION
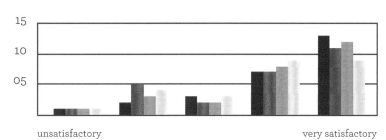

QUALITY OF INTERIOR AIR
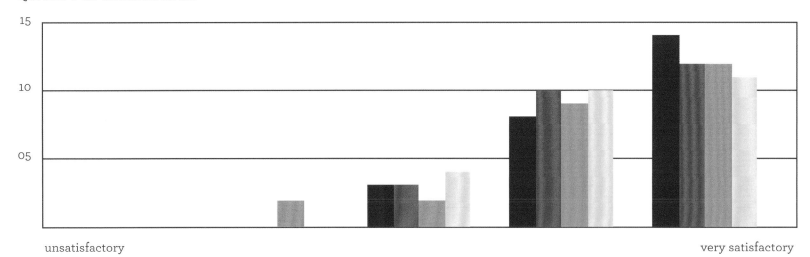

■ lounge ■ bedroom(s) ■ kitchen ■ bathroom

Public housing, Savonnerie Heymans [042]: respecting the historic site was also an important value of the project, just as the preservation of the old reconditioned chimney for ventilating the garages. The overall site forms "a small town with very varied typologies" (MDW architectes).

Jean-François Kleykens,
delegated promoter

[TESTIMONY]
MAKING A CLEAN SWEEP OF THE PAST...
RUE DE LA POSTE [087]

In this neighbourhood of Schaerbeek with its high density housing, it was something of a black sheep. A corner building abandoned for years, squatted for a certain time, and that nobody wanted. An eyesore and a blot on the landscape. Hence the temptation to turn it into a model. This has not been without difficulty.

"Among the population we deal with you find people who are already far from familiar with central heating and the most elementary regulation technology like thermostats and thermostatic valves. How do you expect such people to familiarize themselves from one day to the next with double-flow ventilation?"

It has taken years. First, to convince the owner, little tempted to renovate a cramped living area or to transfer ownership to the municipality. Then, to build in its place a small single-family home that sets an example in a neighbourhood that is in no hurry for a makeover.

The fact is that the building's location is far from ideal. Jean-Francois Kleykens, boss of Renovas and Municipality of Schaerbeek delegate for neighbourhood contracts knows something about this: "If many such buildings are in distress, it is precisely because these are architecturally difficult situations: small living area, large façade, high renovation costs, etc. In this municipality, over the past fifteen years, a vast majority of the renovations we have been involved with relate to corner buildings!"

Yet it is this building that, given its visibility in the neighbourhood, will point to the way of the future: it will be passive. Which ipso facto forces us to demolish. In its place we will erect a light reconstruction (wood frame) using the old foundations. Why? Because in this part of Brussels, no engineering office is going to risk proposing a new building without ensuring its stability by ramming a series of piles into the ground. "If the primary purpose of the neighbourhood contract was only to create new housing, it is certainly not on this type of plot that we would have done it. Here the priority was to remove an eyesore and then to satisfy the 'housing' objective of the neighbourhood contract."

So the adventure started, through the correct procedure of a call for tenders. The contractor who was awarded the contract had no real experience of this type of project. "After six months, it became clear that he was not up to it. He had clearly failed to assess the implications and impositions of passive building. He presented his quotes without having all the cards in his hands in terms of his subcontractors who, as work progressed, systematically communicated prices that exceeded his estimates, forcing him to seek post-haste a cheaper alternative." More lost time!

A new contractor was called upon to continue the site. But deadlines exploded. Scheduled for January 2011, the reception of the site was still not in sight a year later.

Jean-François Kleykens also sees the project as a good example of the way any project that is a little bit innovative can run afoul of public procurement regulations: "For the choice of engineering office, this does not pose too many problems, since we can perform an initial quality selection requiring them to first demonstrate their capacities, with supporting references. For the entrepreneur it is much more difficult, even with detailed specifications. And I am not even speaking of the cases where one wants to use a given eco-material. The same applies for ecological deconstruction/demolition and recycling: it is difficult to fit these into public procurement specifications, especially as these methods are generally time-consuming and neighbourhood contract deadlines are short. We must therefore wait for this approach to become commonplace for a simple technical description to be sufficient to bring to light the right partners."

Renovation of the Mommaerts workshops, Rue Comte de Flandre [022]: wedged between adjoining properties, the Mommaerts renovation has been unable to insulate the façades. Net heating need has been reduced to 58 kWh/m²/year (against an average of 150 kWh/m²/year in the Brussels-Capital Region) (CERAU architectes).

07/ AND ECONOMIC REPLICABILITY?

It is difficult to have a reasonable financial approach in the construction industry: prices are very high, as much for a Batex as for a ruin. Tenant or owner, it is always an obstacle course...

It all depends on the location, both for the price of the land and the cost of work, especially regarding access for the enterprises and their site equipment. The question also depends on labour costs, the price of materials and... the sector's apprehensions. Even the largest agencies have found themselves at one time or another with an estimate twice as high as expected... because the construction company had built in an excessive "safety" margin.

In the first analysis, everyone understands that a small project will cost proportionately more than a large one: small buildings are less compact and more expensive to insulate. Everything depends also on the project: new or renovation, simple or luxurious, efficient or not, etc.

DEFINING AN "ACCEPTABLE" ADDITIONAL COST

Test-Achats has identified the "acceptable" additional cost (without subsidy) for a passive building[1]. Energy savings free up an additional repayment capacity, making it possible to borrow more to cover this extra cost. "We see that several scenarios leave an appreciable margin. Between a basic building (PEB) and a passive construction, we can allocate 170 to 300 €/m² more[2]." It is in renovation that the supplementary budget for passive is naturally the highest: "This money will obviously not be thrown out of the window, because these are also the projects requiring the heaviest resources to attempt to achieve such performance levels [...] But if we consider only the benefit from the removal of a

radiator distribution system, a calculation based on recent builders' estimates shows a gain of 30 to 40 €/m², on top of the above amounts[3]." All of this argues in favour of major renovation, for going as far as possible in the direction of passive building.

BATEX COSTS

The review of the construction costs announced by the winners tends to show that, taking into account the disparities between the different projects, the average cost of construction of a single dwelling (€ 1503/m²) is slightly lower than that of a single non-passive dwelling (€ 1514/m²). This difference is more marked in collective accommodation, with € 1350/m² in passive against € 1494/m² in non-passive. Community amenities built to the passive standard are also cheaper (€ 1582/m²) on average than non-passive ones (€ 1669/m²). In particular, passive building is more expensive in renovation than in new construction, regardless of the destination of the building. It is also more expensive on average for new offices, with € 1565/m² for passive buildings, against € 1492/m² for non-passive ones. Of course other factors also weigh on the overall construction cost of each project and these comparisons are indicative only.

THE PAY-BACK TIME

The evidence shows that the order of priorities – particularly in individual housing[4] – is adapted to the financial constraints. In the commercial sector, the involvement of several property development and property management companies

makes it possible to check how their business model fits the profile of Batex buildings, both for construction and for sale and lease. For example Aéropolis II [040] was built for € 1300/m² (excl. VAT, excluding fees) or a surcharge of 4 to 5% with a pay-back period of 5 years. For Elia [020] the return on investment is 5 years on energy measures, and 8 years overall, with premiums included in the calculations. Based on this experience, the new Elia project for Monnoyer [141] includes an estimated add-on investment of between 3.5 and 8%, with a payback period of 6 to 8 years. The Science-Montoyer offices [107], with an added charge of 9.5%, arrive at a pay-back period of under 10 years[5]. For engineer Alain Bossaer, commercial players "see sufficient benefits to undertake a passive construction, also in economically difficult times[6]."

We can observe the enthusiasm of public housing companies for Batex and the fact that the cost of making their dwellings sustainable and Batex is not much more than the usual construction costs. This is especially true for large operations, less for small, especially those having an experimental dimension.

[1] Olivier Lesage, "Des moyens supplémentaires à investir", in be.passive 09, October 2011, p. 50-51.
[2] The amounts given here are with all taxes and costs included.
[3] In the case of Brussels, where the study was for a detached house, by definition more energy-consuming that a "town" house, we should probably** reduce the financial margin generated by energy savings. This is also the problem of all economic optimum studies: they determine the "master-purchase" of the pavilion model, which we know to be the worst possible model in terms of sustainability…
[4] See the interview with Litte Froonickx and Benjamin Clarysse [122], p. 98-99.
[5] See the interview with Rikkert Leeman [107], p. 154-155.
[6] Interview with Alain Bossaer, "Arcadis Belgium", be.passive 07, April 2011, p. 48.

Passive social housing on Rue de la Plume [035]: the alignments, lines of sight and direction of the individual housing units have been carefully adjusted to give each tenant good access, ample light and the right distance from neighbours (B612 architectes).

Passive nursery on the Rue de l'Hectolitre [153]: on a cramped city centre plot, large south-facing terraces are planned for the children. The compactness of the building and its insulation enable it to achieve the passive standard (R²D² architects).

COST OF OCCUPANCY

Clearly, a more economical building generates cost savings. But the investor also needs to recoup his investment, with reduced charges partially offset by a higher rent. For rented social accommodation, the Region plans to adapt the existing legislation to introduce the concept of occupancy cost[1], this being the "sum of the rent or repayment of the mortgage and the energy costs". This adaptation aims to share the added value arising from the fact of living in passive public housing, with half of the energy savings for the tenants, and the other half being pooled for the benefit of all other tenants.

Project size, the floors and ceilings for subsidies and de *minimis* rule are combined so that the impact of Batex on the financial system varies. The theoretical subsidy of € 100/m² is actually arrived at only in individual housing, even if it is sometimes perceived as inadequate for very small programmes. The average effective subsidy is € 73/m² in collective housing, € 69/m² in amenities buildings and € 51/m² in office buildings. It is here that we can see that some very large projects, such as the 20 000 m² of Belliard [142], are looking to Batex more for the "label" than the subsidies (which represent here only 1.2 % of the construction cost, or € 15/m²).

FROM "PILOT" TO "MATURE" PROJECTS

With a budget of € 24 million over four Batex calls for projects, the regional subsidy corresponds to 6-7 years of energy consumption savings. Other aspects of sustainable building can generate further benefits in terms of health, water consumption, etc[2].

A study has been launched by Brussels Environment of the technical and financial aspects of Batex projects. This should help pinpoint the "sustainability" portion in the overall cost. Based on both actual costs (invoices) and firm offers, Brussels Environment found in the first analysis that the initial additional cost has fallen from 20 to 30% in 2007 to a few percent in 2011. We are moving from "pilot" projects to a second generation of "mature" or "standard" projects. The dynamics of learning and the dedramatizaton of the demands of passive building have no doubt much to do with this. On the other hand, for engineer Alain Bossaer, energy requirements in passive housing are so reduced as to make it difficult to obtain a payback on individual heating systems using renewable energy. "We need to wait for a scale effect and move towards economically more attractive collective systems[3]."

The first results of the satisfaction survey conducted by Brussels Environment show that occupants are fairly satisfied with the cost/benefit ratio, both as tenants (ratio of charges to rent) and as owners.

[1] Bernard Deprez, "Green économie du projet", in *be.passive* 09, October 2011, p. 48.
[2] See the "Value for Money" feature article, in *be.passive* 09, October 2011, p. 48-54.
[3] Interview with Alain Bossaer, "Arcadis", in *be.passive* 07, April 2011, p. 48.

COSTS

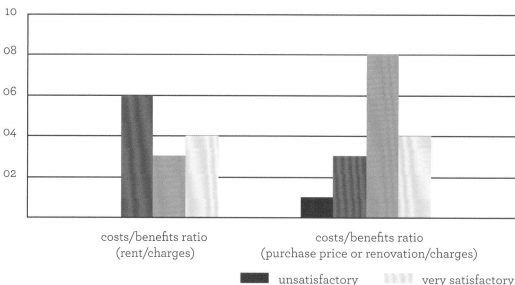

costs/benefits ratio (rent/charges)

costs/benefits ratio (purchase price or renovation/charges)

■ unsatisfactory   ▨ very satisfactory

Passive social housing on Avenue des Familles [133]: this 12-dwelling project in Forest offers human-scale integration into the city, with quality architecture, replicable in many disaffected parts of Brussels (B612 architectes).

Passive floating hotel on Quai des Péniches [113]: the heating and electricity needs of the Hôtel Atlantis will be met by a pellet-fired cogeneration system. In summer a heat pump will recover the coolness of the canal water. The hotel will also be water-autonomous, with water drawn from the canal and purified into drinking water. After filtration, waste water will return to the canal (A2M architectes).

08/ AND THE ARCHITECTURAL AND URBAN QUALITY?

The specificity of the Batex call for projects is its hyper-contextuality. We do not live in a utopia. All projects lead us back to the real, closely built and heavily populated city. The call for Batex projects contains tightly framed requirements and leaves relatively little room for manoeuvre!

The pursuit of the objectives of wellness and energy efficiency point again to the importance of urban bioclimatics, producing highly contemporary solutions that are the very antithesis of stereotypical architecture. Conversely, renovation leaves at times less room for architectural innovation. Architect Marc Opdebeek asks: "Some architects see Batex as a matter for specialists in insulation or renewable technologies... A question of construction and not architecture! This raises the question: should architecture be considered as an independent discipline, essentially artistic in essence, or rather as a way of serving a sustainable society? There is no unanimity on Batex here." Between the posture of "permanent sneering" and that of sincere questioning there are many intermediate shades. Architect Pierre Blondel "is surprised that the focus is in particular on the environmental issue in its consumerist aspect: more insulation, more technology [...] and more regulations... Rather, we should have a reductionist approach: less individual plots, less detached housing... Densifying the existing fabric would [in my opinion] be much more useful than legislating on PEB." Brussels, as a capital city, probably suffers a little less than others from this type of uneconomic use of land. But it could be denser and more compact and better integrate natural green areas. This is one of the urbanization challenges of the Bruyn neighbourhood of northern Brussels.

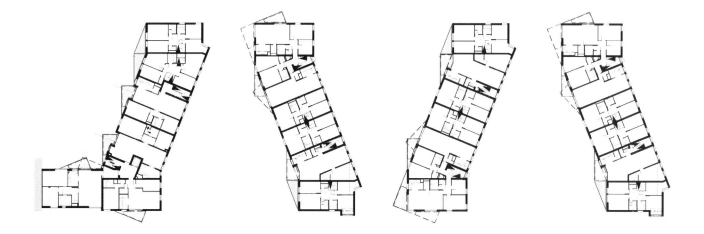

[BATEX 100
— "BRUYN OUEST" SOCIAL HOUSING PROJECT][1]

parcelles cadastrées, 6b, 7, 8, 9b at 1120 Neder-Over-Heembeek | CPAS de la Ville de Bruxelles | Pierre Blondel Architectes sprl | MK Engineering sprl

THE PERMEABLE CITY

Under its 1000 Homes plan, the City of Brussels CPAS/OCMW has launched the building of an ensemble of 79 passive dwellings and a multipurpose hall, in a project entrusted to architect Pierre Blondel. This is an essential element of the future northern neighbourhood of Neder-Over-Heembeek, which the CPAS/OMCW wants to see develop into a "sustainable neighbourhood".

LINKING INHABITANTS AND THE SITE

The architect makes up for an indifferent environment by a subtle siting that is attentive to the welfare of future occupants, to light and to oblique views. Five buildings of 16 units each alternate, forming spaces opening up at times onto the street, at other times onto a nearby natural area. In this way people are prevented from looking onto each other's balconies by means of lateral movements that permit "permeability" between the street and the natural park and invite you to cross the space between the south-west facing apartment blocks and the bottoms of the private gardens.

THE FUNDAMENTALS OF WELL-BEING

This arrangement also ensures excellent natural lighting for the buildings, with the larger distance to adjacent buildings for the higher blocks (R+3) providing the sunlight that passive homes require. The buildings are constructed of sand-lime blocks and insulated from the outside. They are finished in alternating materials, of various colours. The global insulation level is high (K15) and the heating requirement is reduced to an average 12.6 kWh/m².

Each building has centralized ventilation, with supplemental heat provided from the boiler room by a radiator placed on the air pump unit and heated by a condensing boiler. Each tenant is able to refine his personal setting by means of an electric radiator. The hot water for bathrooms is 28% covered by solar collectors.

SUSTAINABLE APPROACH TO THE GROUND AND LANDSCAPE

75 parking spaces are scattered across the site, either outside or half buried and covered with a planted grating. 87 bicycle parking spaces are also provided. Lifts provide disabled access.

The resulting urban permeability is matched by the permeability of the ground, with extensive use of dolomite and turf for the surroundings and private roads and a maximum of green areas. Rainwater management takes on a landscape function, with an open storm basin of a draining model to be built in the park to collect the overflow from the tanks fed by the various roofs. This water will be carried at ground level along open channels along to the footpaths. The water will slowly seep into the soil so as to reduce to zero the discharges of rainwater from the site to the drains.

[1] Read the report in be.passive 09, October 2011, p. 69, and June 2012.

Grouped housing on Avenue Van Volxem [097]: the Brutopia project has arisen from a shared desire of thirty men and women, some from the provinces, to live in Brussels in a way that is at once sustainable, collective and environmentally responsible. The acquisition of a plot of land, the joint construction without a promoter, the joint purchasing of personal finishing materials (kitchen, bathroom, etc.) and everything that can be done on a DIY basis, bring down the prices and make this project feasible (Stekke + Fraas architectes, AAAA architects).

09/ ARCHITECTURE VERSUS SUSTAINABILITY

Must we choose between the environment and architecture? The prize-winners are convinced that the answer is a definite no: the quality of one is not to be gained at the expense of the mediocrity of the other or vice versa. If architecture is against sustainability, it is "against all"[1]. And while there is no contradiction, there is, however, paradox.

The environmental discourse is part of a rationality based on the best scientific advances. It promotes well-mastered technical means, carries regulatory requirements (including obligations both of effort and result, and the identification of collective and reproducible solutions) and aims to reshape the ethical imagination (inducing enthusiasm in some, guilt or denial among others). It is true that by dint of wanting to articulate everything, this discourse of "sustainable construction" may give (itself) the impression of providing a complete, integrated, "holistic" vision of things.

However, from their creative practice, architects intuitively know that the sum of all the criteria of sustainable construction is not enough to "make architecture".

Indeed, architecture invites our attention when "something happens" outside the scope of rational concepts, utility, uses and values. The architecture itself is neither sustainable nor unsustainable: it is what emerges (or not) when "everything" is there and yet there is still something lacking, or – the same thing said a different way – when something more than "everything" is there too. Pointing indifferently towards enjoyment or anxiety, architecture speaks of a gap that cannot be filled: not an indication of "too little", but that of an "overflow" that cannot be contained. In short, like all art forms, it is what the navel is to the body: both scar and indicator of otherness.

Socially and formally speaking, good architecture remains available to what maintains its existence outside the framework which determines it, whether functionality, urban planning regulations or the requirements of sustainable construction.

[1] Bernard Deprez, "Architecture contre durabilité ? Contre… tout contre !", *Les Cahiers de l'Urbanisme n° 66*, December 2007, Région Wallonne, Mardaga.

Espoir passive homes, Rue Fin [060]: designed for the needs of each family, the lower duplexes run right through the building: accessible from the street to the south, they have gardens to the rear. The upper duplexes are accessible by private staircases and offer wide balconies. The architect has responded with an intentionally "non-expert" colour palette to participants' desires for distinct "houses" (D. Carnoy, architect).

10/ GOOD BATEX ARCHITECTURE

Good Batex architecture would in this way be architecture that does not refer to the Batex framework, does not go beyond it or fail to meet it, but refers to an "elsewhere": to the realness of the material world, in both its brutality and its fragility, to the enjoyment of light, the seduction of a material, to the proximity of one's neighbour, to the beauty of the sky, to the uncertainty of passing time, the unbearable lightness of "being alive".

In short, it would be architecture precisely in its ability to make us forget where it came from – the commission – and what it is – use – even if this is exemplary, in its ability to allow an oblique look or gesture, a diversion, a gap, an attractive escape. By introducing "play", it allows everyone to exist by decoupling from the reality of physical and social laws. In this sense architecture is essential because without it we would dwell like ants.

Of course, the Batex political project is played out on a rational plane and it is there that it has all its value. Not only does it not prevent the emer-gence of architecture, but it has integrated it as a dimension of its assessment. It lays the frame-work within which architects will find new short-cuts and permit other oblique looks. This is its limit and this is its strength. The battle is not solely architectural, nor solely environmental: it is cultural. 156 local projects do not make up a comprehensive policy: they install a common space in which to think more globally and they push us to imagine other possibilities. Ultimately, it is the combined experience of all these projects that feeds the initiatives introduced today in the Brussels-Capital Region.

IN THE WORDS
OF AN ARCHITECT

"Thanks to the demand for
architectural quality and technical
efficiency and the criteria of
reproducibility and profitability, the
exemplary buildings effectively
provide a source of inspiration
for new projects."
Engineer Bram De Meester

"The great majority of the projects
which have been selected deserve to
be, and have a definite illustrative
value. The question is whether
Batex should be held annually and
indefinitely. Is there not a danger
of the quality and degree of
innovation of projects levelling off,
after a number of editions?"
Architect Marc Opdebeek

11/ AND IF WE HAD
TO DO IT ALL OVER AGAIN?

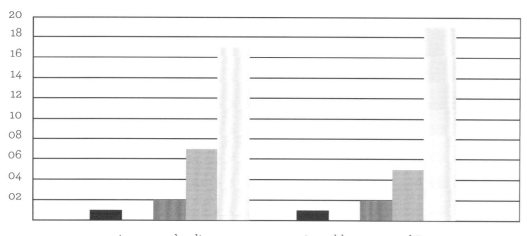

i am proud to live
in an exemplary building

i would recommend Batex

 unsatisfactory   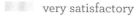 very satisfactory

Building passive on Avenue des Courses [089]: the homes are well-lit, with right-through apartments totally open to the front. Single-direction studios benefit from a frontage of 9.90 m. The orientation and location allow them to make full use of sunlight to minimize costs (MDW architecture).

IN THE WORDS OF AN ARCHITECT

"We have tried to avoid the 'one-shot', aiming rather at an architectural project that can serve as a replicable model in the European market in terms of comfort, flexibility and cost. Four years later, this motivation is still one of our driving forces. The Batex seal gives us a certain credibility to begin with. Afterwards, we have to give concrete shape, and it is only the quality of our work that enables us not to lose this credibility."
Architect Sabine Leribaux

"Currently we are integrating these concerns into all our projects. 100% of our projects could compete in the Batex call for projects."
Architect Olivier Mathieu

"When I see the impact on the profession and the sector, I'm 1000% for Batex, like all my colleagues."
Architect Sebastian Moreno-Vacca

"This is an extraordinary opportunity we had to push the thinking process so far – and we intend to share this experience. We will be back soon!"
Architect Sebastian Cruyt

Passive house on Rue Verrewinkel [083]: the first project of this kind for the architects; they wanted to design a detached house to reach the passive criterion. They also state that "these sustainable intentions are inseparable from the desire to offer a quality contemporary architecture based on natural light and on quality living spaces" (P. Blondel, architect).

TOOLS

[GLOSSARY]
[INDEXES]
[REFERENCE DOCUMENTS]
[GUIDANCE
AND SUPPORT SERVICES]

[GLOSSARY]

BIODIVERSITY*
The taking into account of the characteristics of the site in terms of plant cover (maintenance/strengthening of the existing plant cover), biodiversity* (native species), topography and hydrography.

BLOWER-DOOR*
See n50.

BREEAM*
British Research Establishment Environmental Assessment Method: environmental certification of buildings delivered by the UK Building Research Establishment, www.BREEAM.org

CANADIAN WELL / PROVENCE WELL
This is an air intake device by which air is introduced into the building through a pipe placed in the ground; in this way the incoming air is heated in winter (because the ground is warmer than the air) and cooled in summer (because the ground is cooler than the air) in a passive way.

COMFORT
Particular attention is paid to issues of health and comfort:
– acoustic comfort, using for example acoustic glazing, low-noise technical installations and/or higher performance insulation of technical rooms, sound insulation of ducts and false ceilings, etc.
– visual comfort, with an emphasis on natural light and ensuring the quality of artificial lighting.
– quality of indoor air: in addition to energy-related aspects, ventilation is designed to ensure good indoor air quality (humidity, temperature, odours, etc.). Where applicable, the ventilation system includes an air filtration unit, which needs to be maintained by a specialized firm. The relative air humidity is between 50 and 70%.
– summer comfort: design of cooling (active or passive) to ensure a comfortable temperature in summer. Measures are taken to prevent overheating in summer.

CO-HOUSING
Form of grouped habitat with an accent on user-friendliness, joint organisation, cost saving and pooling of resources.

COMMISSIONING
The mission of commissioning is the initial follow-up of a building, just after reception. For one or two years, a mandated agent records and analyses the consumption and comfort level of the building in order to optimize all parameters.

COMPACTNESS
This is the ratio between volume and heat loss surface area. Compactness is influenced by size (large buildings are more compact than small ones), shape (a cube is more compact than a more complex volume) and the urban typology (heat is not lost through party walls). The more compact a building, the less the energy loss, all other things being equal. A building that lacks compactness requires better insulation.

DOUBLE-FLOW VENTILATION WITH HEAT RECOVERY
This is controlled mechanical ventilation (CMV) with 2 fans with a flow of incoming fresh air and a flow of exhaust air. The heat recovery takes the form of a device that allows the flows to cross without mixing, so that up to 95% (yield η of the installation) of the energy contained in the exhaust air can be transferred to the incoming air. These exchangers are essential for reducing energy needs beyond the low energy standard.

E

The E index is a percentage (unitless) measuring the ratio between the primary energy need of a building and that of a reference building defined by the government according to the building standards in force in 2000. For example, a building with an index E90 means that its primary energy need is 90% of the reference building.
The Regions define the Emax values that may not be exceeded.

ECO-MATERIALS

Ecological materials minimize the negative impact on health and the environment.
These are materials that are locally sourced and/or recycled and/or low in embodied energy (energy that is necessary for the production and deconstruction of materials), which do not present a hazard to health. These include, for example, labelled materials, or categories 1a to 3c of the NIBE reference framework, materials guaranteed CFC/HCFC free, etc. The project design takes into consideration the flexibility of use of the building and its premises, and the durability and ease of maintenance of the chosen building materials.

ECO-MOBILITY

This defines the match between the destination of the building and its accessibility by public transport and soft mobility (walking, cycling). Properly sized bike parking facilities are provided, as well as showers and lockers for cyclists at the workplace. Access is easy within the building or complex for persons with reduced mobility.

EFFLUENT

Household waste water: used water, excluding black water.
Grey water: weakly charged waste water (storm water, rainwater, household waste water).
Black water: faecal water.

EMBODIED ENERGY

The embodied energy of a material or product is the energy necessary for its production, transportation and deconstruction.

ENERGY STANDARDS IN THE BRUSSELS-CAPITAL REGION

A low energy building has a net energy need (BEN) $\leq$ 60 kWh/m^2 per year.
A very low energy building has a net energy need $\leq$ 30 kWh/m^2 per year.
A passive building presents a net energy need $\leq$ 15 kWh /m^2 per year (For the other criteria, see Chapter 3).
A zero energy building is passive and has offsets its energy requirements (heating and electricity) by local energy production based on renewable energy.
A positive energy building is a passive building that produces and passes renewable energy into the grid in greater quantity than the energy it takes from it.

FOSSIL ENERGY

Fossil energy comes from limited resources: coal, oil and gas, which produce carbon dioxide (CO_2). Uranium is not a fossil fuel, but is non-renewable.

GREEN ROOFS

The greening of roofs slows rainwater runoff and reduces excessive runoff and flooding during storms. It also protects the waterproofing of the roof. It comprises a sealing and a complex for plants to grow on the surface. It can be intensive (depth of soil permitting growing of grass, with the roof being accessible to humans) or extensive (thin layer of substrate for the development of succulent plants, the roof is not then accessible).

HEALTH

See Comfort.

HEAT PUMP

A heat pump uses the energy found naturally in soil, air or water as a reservoir (cold source); the pump uses electricity to compress and circulate a fluid that absorbs the heat contained in the cold source and transfers it to the room to be heated. A heat pump is said to be "reversible" if it is capable of operating also in the other direction, that is to say, to produce cold (like a refrigerator).

INFILTROMETER

See: n50

INSULATION

The insulation of a building is provided by the choice of materials having a low heat conductance. This conductance is estimated by the parameter U (W/m^2K): it is the energy power lost (or gained) per m^2 and per difference of one degree between inside and outside.

IPCC

Intergovernmental Panel on Climate Change, www.ipcc.ch

K

The average insulation level K characterizes the ability of a building to transmit heat through its walls (W/K) and is calculated by weighting the impact of all the walls. The lower the K, the better insulated the building.
The Regions define Kmax values that may not be exceeded.

kWh/m^2 PER YEAR

A kWh is the amount of energy.
The kWh per m^2 per year measures the specific energy needs (e.g. for heating) per 1 m^2 of the building and for an entire heating season (1 year). This unit permits comparison between different sized buildings. The same measure can be used to compare actual consumption levels.

LAGOONING

This is a way of purifying waste water by the action of plants, oxygen and sunlight in outdoor ponds.

N50

This value serves to measure the airtightness of a building. Very high performance buildings need to control and prevent losses via drafts by being very airtight. This airtightness is measured by an infiltrometric or blower-door® test that checks the flow of air entering/exiting through cracks when maintaining a pressure difference of 50 Pa between inside and outside.

NET HEATING REQUIREMENT (FRENCH: BEN_{ch})

Net amount of energy needed for heating; see Operating energy.

NIBE

The NIBE (Dutch Institute for Construction Biology and Ecology) offers a classification of building materials based on their ecological criteria as a function of a life cycle analysis. The classification incorporates measurable data (energy consumption, emissions, etc.) and other more qualitative factors (landscape degradation, pollution, health, etc.). Eco-materials belong to NIBE categories 1, 2 and 3; materials belonging to the last 3 NIBE categories (5, 6 and 7) are to be disallowed.

OPERATING ENERGY

This is the energy consumed for the normal use of the buildings. In construction, we compute three forms of energy:
– Net Heating Need (in French: BEN_{ch}): this is the amount of energy needed to produce the heat which the occupant needs in order to be comfortable, taking into account the thermal quality of the building. This parameter provides information on the quality of building design.
– Final energy consumption: the Net Heating Need increased by the energy lost by the heating or cooling system. This is energy (fuel oil, electricity, etc.) that you have to buy. This parameter takes into account the thermal quality of the building and its technical facilities.
– Primary energy (EP) consumption: this takes into account (via conversion factors) of all losses due to the intermediate transformation processes; this parameter permits the aggregation of all energy consumptions.

PASSIVE COOLING

In Batex, passive strategies are devised to manage potential overheating problems without consuming energy. Passive cooling avoids the use of active air conditioning. These strategies combine and use sunscreens (mobile or fixed), Canadian wells, intensive natural ventilation, night cooling, etc.

PEB

Transposed from a European Directive, the Energy Performance Requirements for Buildings (in French: PEB) establishes a process for calculating the E index. The PEB is complemented by regional decrees setting the maximum value. The PEB has been applicable in Brussels since 2008.

PHP

Passiefhuis Platform,
www.passiefhuisplatform.be

PHPP

In Batex application files, the Net Energy Need is calculated using the PHPP software developed since 1991 by the Passivhaus Institut (Darmstadt) and/or with the help of a dynamic simulation program.

PMP

Plateforme Maison passive,
www.maisonpassive.be

RENEWABLE ENERGIES

They are available in unlimited quantities and come from the sun (thermal and photovoltaic), wind (wind farms), the water cycle (hydroelectric dams) and the plant cycle (wood, biomass and biofuels).

SOLAR PANEL

There are two families of solar panels:
- Photovoltaic cells convert solar energy into electricity, a PV system is characterized by a peak power, reached in full sunlight;
- Thermal panels convert solar energy into heat for heating domestic sanitary water or for domestic heating.

THERMOGRAPHY

A technology that uses an infrared camera to visualize wall temperatures and identify defects in the insulation of buildings.

TRIAS ENERGETICA

Strategy of designing high energy-efficiency buildings: the need for heating energy is first reduced by optimizing the thermal insulation and the airtightness of the building, the solar gain and energy recovery. The balance is covered by fossil fuels using the technically most effective installations possible or renewable energy that does not produce CO_2.

U

Thermal conductance U characterizes the ability of a wall to transmit a flow or heat (W/m^2K): the lower the U, the better the wall is insulated.
The Regions define Umax values that may not be exceeded.

WASTE

Waste management concerns first of all the management of the building site: minimizing waste production (limiting the extent of demolition work, sorting and reuse of demolished materials, etc.). Waste that cannot be recycled on-site is sorted and guided towards recycling industries. Waste management also covers the management of waste created when the building is in use: including in the project devices enabling easy sorting of waste and, where appropriate, reuse or recycling in situ or in the vicinity.

WATER

Water management comprises different aspects:
– limiting water use focuses on the actions and installations that limit water consumption, for example pressure reducing valves, flow restrictor taps, double-flush or stop-button toilets, water saving shower heads, etc.
– management and recovery of rainwater aimed at reducing urban runoff with features minimizing impervious surfaces and grey areas (access roads, parking lots etc. in permeable hard surfaces), devices permanently removing rainwater from runoff (infiltration), green roofs, etc.
– grey water management: this is the local treatment of grey water and runoff so as not to reject these waters directly into the natural environment.

ZERO CARBON

This concept is based, on the one hand, on the reduction of energy requirements (heating, electricity, etc.) and, on the other hand, on the use of renewable energies that do not emit CO_2 (solar, wind, biomass) in order to cover the operating energy requirements.

[INDEXES]
[INDEX OF PROJECTS]

[# BATEX] NAME | ADDRESS | PROJECT OWNER | ARCHITECT | DESIGN OFFICE

[001] Maison de la jeunesse L'Avenir | Chaussée d'Anvers 156 at 1000 Bruxelles | Ville de Bruxelles | R²D² Architecture sa | Détang sa > *124*, 126

[002] Ecole Emile Bockstael | Rue du Heysel 104 at 1020 Laeken | Ville de Bruxelles | NVT architekten | Schmidt Reuter > 139

[003] Van Soust | Rue Van Soust 449 at 1070 Anderlecht | Maloteau, Alexandre and Frederique | Alexis Versele architecte | Lippens

[004] Crèche Gaucheret | Rue Rogier at 1030 Schaerbeek | Commune de Schaerbeek | MDW Architecture | Waterman TCA > *67*, 126, *127*

[005] Crèche n° 9 | Rue du Gulden Bodem 2 at 1080 Molenbeek-Saint-Jean | Commune de Molenbeek-Saint-Jean | A2M sprl | Matriciel > *141*

[006] Telex | Boulevard de l'Impératrice 17-19 at 1000 Bruxelles | Befimmo | Crepain Binst Architecture sa | VK Engineering > 116, *147*, *149* ,*153*, 162, 179

[007] Rodenbach | Avenue Rodenbach at 1030 Schaerbeek | Commune de Schaerbeek | 3A architectes | Ecorce > *82*

[008] Faes | Rue Faes 20 at 1090 Jette | Maison Hubert Cabay sa | Marc Opdebeeck Modelmo | Ally & Be > 146, 168, *169*

[009] Nys | Rue Antoine Nys 86 at 1070 Anderlecht | Architects Office Lahon & Partners | Architects Office Lahon & Partners | 3E > 162, *163*, 184

[010] Hopstraat | Rue du Houblon 47 at 1000 Bruxelles | Huygh Jo, Verhasselt Katleen | AA Ravenstein III

[011] Ferme Nos Pilifs | Trassersweg 347-349 at 1120 Neder-Over-Heembeek | Ferme Nos Pilifs | Jacques Meganck architecte | Matriciel > 30, *31,* 130, 146, *153*, 168

[012] Basse | Rue Basse 90 at 1180 Uccle | Moyaerts-Leblanc | Marc Opdebeeck Modelmo | Ally & Be

[013] Waterloo | Chaussée de Waterloo 1253 at 1180 Uccle | Urbanscape | B612 associates sprl | Matriciel > *54*, 29

[014] Vanpé | Rue Vanpé 50 at 1190 Forest | CPAS de Forest | A2M sprl | Matriciel > 116, 130, *161*, 162, *163*, 179, *187*, *188*

[015] MRS CPAS St Josse | Rue de la Cible 5 at 1210 Saint-Josse-ten-Noode | CPAS de Saint-Josse-ten-Noode | ETAU sprl | Grontmij > *133*, 139, 160

[016] Loossens | Rue Loossens 42 at 1090 Jette | Foyer jettois | A2M sprl | Ecorce > 47, 48, *49, 70, 173,* 176

[017] Wauters | Rue Joseph Wauters 61 at 1030 Schaerbeek | Camacho-Santos Ines, Biondi Anita | Camacho-Santos Inès architecte > *14*, 56, 101, 160, *170*, 184

[018] Dubrucq | Avenue J. Dubrucq 222-224 at 1080 Molenbeek-Saint-Jean | Commune de Molenbeek-Saint-Jean | B-Architecten sprl | Gebotec > *2*, *40*, *45*, *80*, 81

[019] Archiducs | Avenue des Archiducs 74 at 1040 Etterbeek | Henrard Thierry, Piazza Véronique | Thierry Henrard architecte

[020] Bureaux Elia | Avenue de Vilvorde 126 at 1000 Bruxelles | Elia System Operator | Gilson, Libert & Partners sprl | 3E > 20, 30, 150, 198

[021] Montagne Saint-Job | Montagne de Saint-Job 35 at 1180 Uccle | Bedoret Gérard, Damas Véronique | Gérard Bedoret architecte | Gérard Bedoret > *53*, 87, 101, 102, *103*, *188*

[022] Atelier Mommaerts | Rue Comte de Flandre 45-51 at 1080 Molenbeek-Saint-Jean | Commune de Molenbeek-Saint-Jean | CERAU Architects Partners | 3E > *74*, 116, *199*

[023] IMMI | Avenue des Résédas 51 at 1070 Anderlecht | IMMI asbl | TRAIT architects sa | Ecorce, Atelier Chora > 30, 126, 136, *137*

[024] Eenens | Rue Général Eenens 41 at 1030 Schaerbeek | Foyer schaerbeekois | Atelier La Licorne scprl

[025] Caméléon | Avenue Ariane 15 at 1200 Woluwe-Saint-Lambert | Ariane Gestco sa | cw architect sprl | Matriciel > *29*, 30, 146, 168

[026] Albatros Village | Chaussée d'Haecht at 1130 Haren | Immobilien Vennootschap van Vlaanderen nv | Conix Architects scprl | VK Engineering, Matriciel > 176

[027] Galilei | Avenue Van Oss 1 at 1120 Neder-Over-Heembeek | SDRB-Société de Développement de la Région de Bruxelles-Capitale | Modulo Architects sprl | JZH & Partners, 3E

[028] Toutes les couleurs | Avenue de toutes les couleurs 17 at 1200 Woluwe-Saint-Lambert | Commune de Woluwe-Saint-Lambert | Georges Brutsaert Architectes | JZH & Partners à MatriCiel

[029] Van de Woestyne | Rue Léon Van de Woestyne 29 at 1160 Auderghem | Neubourg-Monneaux | Isabelle Prignot architecte | Ecorce

[030] Pikshouse | Rue Richard Piks 20 at 1040 Etterbeek | Collignon Laurent | Laurent Collignon, David Dardenne architectes > 116

[031] Globe | Chaussée d'Alsemberg 774-776 at 1180 Uccle | Green Immo sprl | FHW architectes | Ecorce > 47, 60, 88, *89*

[032] Van Volxem | Avenue Van Volxem at 1190 Forest | JCX Gestion | Art & Build Architect | Arcadis Gedas nv, VK Engineering > 148, 150

[033] Diamant | Avenue du Diamant 71 at 1030 Schaerbeek | Schuijt-Maher | Marc Opdebeeck Modelmo | Ally & Be > *111*, 116, 179, *188*
[034] Midi-Suède | Rue de Suède 24-36 at 1060 Saint-Gilles | DHB sa (SDRB-BPI) | Urban Platform | Daidalos Peutz > *37*, *55*, *73*, 81, 175
[035] Plume | Rue de la Plume at 1000 Bruxelles | Foyer bruxellois | B612 associates sprl | Enesta Engineering, Ecorce > 81, *201*
[036] CHU Brugmann | Rue du Foyer schaerbeekois 36 at 1030 Schaerbeek | Association hospitalière de Bruxelles et de Schaerbeek |
Bureau d'Architecture Emile Verhaegen | Matriciel > *15,* 30, 139
[037] La Ceriseraie | Avenue Urbain Britsiers 11 at 1030 Schaerbeek | CPAS de Schaerbeek | A.A.U. nv | Marcq & Roba > 30, 139
[038] SIAMU | Chaussée d'Haecht at 1030 Schaerbeek | Service d'Incendie et d'Aide médicale urgente de la Région de Bruxelles-Capitale | Hoet,
Minne, Arcoplan association momentanée | Bice, Matriche > 126, 139
[039] Cygnes-Digue | Rue des Cygnes/Rue de la Digue at 1050 Ixelles | Commune d'Ixelles | Lpp Ledroit Pierret Polet, AAO, Label Architecture
> *17*, *36*, 81, 126
[040] Aéropolis II | Avenue Urbain Britsiers at 1030 Schaerbeek | Maison du Travail asbl | Architectes Associés | Cenergie
> 30, 32, *33*, 55, 146, *150*, *161*, 176, 198
[041] Clémenceau | Avenue Clemenceau at 1070 Anderlecht | VK Group | B.A.E.B. sprl | VK Engineering > 150
[042] Savonnerie Heymans | Rue d'Anderlecht 131-147 at 1000 Bruxelles | CPAS de la Ville de Bruxelles | MDW architectes | MK Engineering sprl
> *12*, *53*, 56, 60, 74, *75*, *195*
[043] Rubens | Rubensstraat 92 at 1030 Schaerbeek | Filleul S., De Nys Ann | Ecorce > *100*, *107,* 116
[044] De Vrière | de Vrièrestraat 14 at 1020 Laeken | Van Leeuw – Van Eetvelt | Van Leeuw – Van Eetvelt > 20, *21*, 100
[045] MaisiE | Rue de la Clinique 90 at 1070 Anderlecht | Dal Molin Loik, Sumner Suzy | Dardenne David, Collignon Laurent architectes > *97*, *185*
[046] Droguerie | Chaussée de Forest 96 at 1060 Saint-Gilles | Kirschfink Elin, Leurquin Georges | Gwenola Vilet | Escape + M. Montulet
> *110*, 112, *113*, 130, 179
[047] Stuckens | Rue Edouard Stuckens 58 at 1140 Evere | Hachez-Demoustier Madeline and Gaël | FHW architectes | Ecorce
[048] Leemans | Rue Docteur Leemans 39 at 1082 Berchem-Sainte-Agathe | Van Roy Xavier, Morales Paula | FHW architectes | Ecorce > *96*, *117*
[049] Fléron | Avenue de Fléron 40 at 1190 Forest | Boutry Frédéric, Gulmot Delphine | FHW architectes | Ecorce > *16*, 20
[050] nESt | Rue de la Poterie 19 at 1070 Anderlecht | D'Hellem, Stragier | Nele Stragier (MET architectuur) | Factor 4 > 81, *107*, *109*
[051] Huberti | Rue Gustave Huberti 13 at 1030 Schaerbeek | Alexandre Olivier, Stevelinck Laurence | Alexandre Olivier architecte | Ecorce
> 38, *109*, 116, 118, 120, 122
[052] Lisbonne | Rue de Lisbonne 22 at 1060 Saint-Gilles | Ledroit Anne, Pierret Vincent | Lpp Ledroit – Pierret – Polet | Energipark Reiden
[053] Dix-Arpents | Avenue des dix Arpents 103 at 1200 Woluwe-Saint-Lambert | Strages sa | Atelier 229 sprl | Ally & Be
[054] Besme | Avenue Besme 107-109 at 1190 Forest | Foreign Office & CSI | A-Cube Architecture | Cenergie > 92, 116, *178*, 179, *187*
[055] Biplan | Rue du Biplan at 1130 Haren | Bxleco1 sprl | Bxleco1 sprl, FHW architectes | Bxleco1, Ecorce > 47, 60, 62, *63*
[056] Deux Tours | Rue des Deux Tours 4-8 at 1210 Saint-Josse-ten-Noode | Habitations à Bon Marché de Saint-Josse-ten-Noode |
Atelier d'Architecture Van Oost sprl, Thaddée Van Oost Architecte | Ecorce
[057] Tilleul | Rue du Tilleul 179-187 at 1140 Evere | Commune d'Evere | A2M sprl | A2M sprl > 179
[**058] Gérard** | Rue Gérard 15 at 1040 Etterbeek | Indivision Draps | Edouard Draps architecte | Enesta Engineering > *109*
[059] Delaunoy | Rue Delaunoy 141 at 1080 Molenbeek-Saint-Jean | Société de Promotions Immobilières Durables et Ecologique scrl (SPIDEC) |
Atelier d'Architecture A+A+A+A scrl | Geotech Partners
[060] L'Espoir | Rue Fin 3-13 at 1080 Molenbeek-Saint-Jean | Fonds du Logement scrl | Damien Carnoy Architecte | MK Engineering sprl
> 20, 22, *23*, *36*, 39, *53*, 87, 175, *209*, 211
[061] Florair | Avenue Guillaume Degreef 1-4 at 1090 Jette | Foyer jettois | Atelier d'Architecture Phillipe Segui SPRL | Daidalos Peutz > 20, *21*, 72, 87, 116
[062] Pépin | Rue du Pépin 31-37 at 1000 Bruxelles | Kervyn Guillaume, Boels Lucas | Conix Architects scprl | MK Engineering sprl > 106, 140, *191*

[135] **Lemmens** | Chaussée de Mons 11 at 1070 Anderlecht | Commune d'Anderlecht | Ariade Architectes | ACE
[136] **Harenberg** | Harenberg 115-163 at 1130 Haren | Régie foncière de la Ville de Bruxelles | A2M sprl | Stockman nv > *43*, 47, 60, *69*
[137] **Simons** | Rue Simons at 1000 Bruxelles | Régie foncière de la Ville de Bruxelles | A2M sprl | CREA-TEC sprl > 72, 139, *174*
[138] **Ligue des Familles** | Avenue Emile de Beco 111 at 1050 Ixelles | Ligue des Familles | EURECA sprl > 116
[139] **Byrrh** | Rue Dieudonné Lefèvre 4 at 1020 Laeken | CPAS de la Ville de Bruxelles | JZH & Partners / Ozon architecture/ N. Créplet | Matriciel
> 146, 168, *169*, 179
[140] **Hainaut** | Quai du Hainaut 31-37 at 1080 Molenbeek-Saint-Jean | Commune de Molenbeek-Saint-Jean |
L'Escaut-MSA-Grontmij association momentanée | Enesta Engineering > 140, *141*
[141] **Monnoyer** | Quai Léon Monnoyer 3 at 1000 Bruxelles | Elia System Operator | SCA Architectes Associés | Arcadis Belgium
> 47, 55, 148, 150, 151, *153*, 158, 198
[142] **Belliard** | Rue Belliard 40 at 1040 Etterbeek | Cofinimmo | Art & Build Architect | CES > *26*, *27*, 146, 158, 200
[143] **Navez** | Rue François-Joseph Navez at 43 at 1030 Schaerbeek | Commune de Schaerbeek | Vanden Eeckhoudt-Creyf architectes > 140
[144] **Sceptre** | Rue du Sceptre 13-19 at 1050 Ixelles | Commune d'Ixelles | Pierre Blondel architectes sprl | MK Engineering sprl > 140, *141*
[145] **Bains de Laeken** | Rue du Champ de l'Eglise 73-89 at 1020 Laeken | Ville de Bruxelles | R²D² Architecture sa | JZH & Partners > 140 176
[146] **Association** | Rue de l'Association 14-16 at 1000 Bruxelles | Ville de Bruxelles | R²D² Architecture sa | Matriciel, JZH Partners
[147] **Chazal** | Avenue Chazal 181-183 at 1030 Schaerbeek | Commune de Schaerbeek | ARJM Architecture | JZH & Partners > 139
[148] **Montjoie** | Avenue Montjoie 30 at 1180 Uccle | Institut Marie Immaculée Montjoie asbl | TRAIT architects sa | Atelier Chora > 138, 139
[149] **Rousseau** | Avenue Victor Rousseau 46-48 at 1190 Forest | Institut Sainte-Ursule Pouvoir Organisateur | TRAIT architects sa | Atelier Chora
> *29*, 116, 136
[150] **Merchtem** | Chaussée de Merchtem 9 at 1080 Molenbeek-Saint-Jean | Vier-Winden-Basisschool bvba | Plan A architectenbureau sprl | CES
> 60, 116, 139
[151] **Sextant** | Rue du Sextant 41 at 1082 Berchem-Sainte-Agathe | Commission Communautaire Française | AAC Architecture | Matriche
[152] **Willems** | Place Joseph Benoît Willems 11 at 1020 Laeken | Ville de Bruxelles | TRAIT architects sa > *141*
[153] **Hectolitre** | Rue de l'Hectolitre at 1000 Bruxelles | Ville de Bruxelles | R²D² Architecture sa | Matriciel > *201*
[154] **Arts & Métiers** | Rue de la Rosée 3 at 1070 Anderlecht | Ville de Bruxelles | MDW Architecture | VK Engineering, Enesta Engineering
> 47, 81, 139, *174*
[155] **Wimpelberg** | Rue du Wimpelberg 188 at 1120 Neder-Over-Heembeek | Le Potelier asbl | Pierre Blondel Architectes sprl | MK Engineering sprl > 140
[156] **KOUBA** | Rue Vanderlinden 81-87 at 1030 Schaerbeek | ACIRSP asbl | Huwaert Frédéric | Ecorce > 140

[INDEX OF PROJECT OWNERS]

Mutimmo **[103]**
Nelson Canal sa **[112]**
Neubourg-Monneaux **[029]**
Nicodème Hélène and Tilman Raphaël **[081]**
Pazienza Diego **[129]**
Petit Joëlle, Hauzeur Nicolas **[123]**
R&N Estate sa **[104]**
Roman Séverine, Materna Gérard **[080]**
Commune de Saint-Gilles **[106]**
Commune de Saint-Josse-ten-Noode
[071] [116]
CPAS de Saint-Josse-ten-Noode **[015]**
Habitations à Bon Marché,
Saint-Josse-ten-Noode **[056]**
Commune de Schaerbeek **[004] [007]**
[087] [143] [147]
CPAS de Schaerbeek **[037]**
Foyer schaerbeekois **[024]**
Schuijt-Maher **[033]**
SDRB-Société de Développement de la
Région de Bruxelles-Capitale **[027] [108] [132]**
Sellier Amandine, Vande Perre Marc **[124]**
Service d'Incendie et d'Aide Médicale Urgente
de la Région de Bruxelles-Capitale **[038]**
Service Public Fédéral Mobilité et Transport **[131]**
Simon Charles **[101]**
Sintzoff Marie **[121]**

Société de Promotions Immobilières Durables
et Ecologiques scrl (SPIDEC) **[059]**
Strages sa **[053]**
Commune d'Uccle **[064]**
Urbani sa **[128]**
Urbanscape **[013]**
Van Leeuw – Van Eetvelt **[044]**
Van Roy Xavier, Morales Paula **[058]**
Vandenbulcke Mathias **[118]**
Vier-Winden-Basisschool bvba **[150]**
VK Group **[041]**
Vlaamse Gemeenschapscommissie **[115]**
Commune de Watermael-Boitsfort **[126]**
Winssinger Philippe, Villé Marcel **[089]**
Commune de Woluwe-Saint-Lambert **[028]**

[INDEX OF ARCHITECTS]

[INDEX OF DESIGN OFFICES]

[INDEX OF PEOPLE MENTIONED]

[REFERENCE DOCUMENTS]

INFO SHEETS FOR PROFESSIONALS
Practical guidebook to the sustainable construction and renovation of smaller buildings
www.bruxellesenvironnement.be > Accueil > Professionnels > Themes > Eco-construction
> Guide pratique petits bâtiments (Home page > Professionals > Themes > Eco-construction
> Practical guide to smaller buildings)

The guidebook (in separate French and Dutch editions) covers the sustainable construction and renovation in the five fields listed below, each corresponding to an abbreviation. The recommendations of the guidebook are presented as printable sheets. Although they address different domains, they all have the same structure for easy reading. They provide general answers ("principles"), assist with the design ("elements of sustainable choice"), propose solutions ("implementation") and provide additional information ("information"). The five areas of sustainable construction are:

Areas	Abbreviation	Content
TERRITORY	TER	That which characterizes a sustainable architecture in its relationship to the urban context in terms of opportunities for social interaction, non-motorized mobility, urban landscape and biodiversity*.
ENERGY	ENE	All applications involved in constructing an energy-efficient building, involving the control of energy needs and the choice of systems and energy sources to meet them.
WATER	EAU (WATER)	The resources for integrated water management including its judicious use, its depollution and use of rainwater to position the architecture better within the water cycle.
MATERIALS	MAT	Actions to be taken – from the ecological choice of materials to the management of waste – in order to achieve an architecture that takes into account the finiteness of resources throughout its life cycle.
HEALTH AND COMFORT	CSS (H&C)	All the provisions that ensure the architecture of building aligns with its use in terms of health, comfort and space configuration for renewed living pleasure.

ECO-BUILDING INFO SHEETS FOR INDIVIDUALS

www.bruxellesenvironnement.be > Home page > Individuals > Themes > Eco-construction
> Our info sheets (Accueil > Particuliers > Thèmes > Eco-construction > Nos info-fiches)

Action-oriented, eco-construction info sheets (in French and Dutch) have been prepared, covering many topics of sustainable construction, to help people make the right choices before starting work.

ENERGY INFO SHEETS FOR INDIVIDUALS

www.bruxellesenvironnement.be > Accueil > Particuliers > Thèmes > Eco-construction
> Nos info-fiches (Home page > Individuals > Themes > Eco-construction > Our info sheets)

A hundred or so info sheets (in French and Dutch) are devoted specifically to energy, covering topics as diverse as the choice of a boiler, the points of attention when buying a home, insulation of a flat or inclined roof, etc.

EXEMPLARY BUILDINGS INFO SHEETS

www.bruxellesenvironnement.be > Accueil > Particuliers > Thèmes > Eco-construction
> Bâtiments Exemplaires > Publications (> Home page > Individuals > Themes
> Eco-construction > Exemplary buildings > Publications)

These info sheets (in French and Dutch) address the essential themes of "eco-performance". They set out to share good practices that have already been implemented and which are applicable in various sustainable projects. The following info sheets are downloadable in PDF format:

Info sheet 1.1: Airtightness (L'étanchéité à l'air)
Info sheet 1.2: Airtightness (L'étanchéité à l'air)
Info sheet 2.1: Double-flow ventilation in individual and collective housing (no translation?)
Info sheet 2.2: The design of artificial lighting for housing and offices (La conception de l'éclairage artificiel dans les logements et les bureaux)
Info sheet 3.1: Free cooling via intensive ventilation (le free-cooling par ventilation intensive)
Info sheet 3.2: Comparison of heating and sanitary hot water systems for individual houses and apartment blocks in passive design and low energy renovation. (Comparatif des systèmes de chauffage et ECS pour les maisons individuelles et les immeubles à appartements en conception passive et rénovation basse énergie)
Info sheet 3.3: Overheating risks (Les risques de surchauffe)
Info sheet 4.1: Use of recycled granulates (L'utilisation de granulats issus du recyclage)
Info sheet 4.2: Compatibility between solar panels and the design of green roofs
(La compatibilité entre les panneaux solaires et la conception des toitures vertes)
Info sheet 4.3: Waste management in the construction sector (La gestion des déchets du secteur de la construction)

[GUIDANCE AND SUPPORT SERVICES]

SERVICES FOR PROFESSIONALS
Sustainable Building Facilitator Service
www.bruxellesenvironnement.be/facilitateur
The Building Facilitator's office is available on a permanent basis to offer general guidance on all topics relating to the management, renovation or construction of a building in a sustainable manner. The service is available to professionals working in building in the Brussels Region, in the public sector, commercial companies, non-commercial organizations, property management (apartments over 1 000 m² or more than 10 apartments) and condominiums.
Contact: Tel. 0800 85 775 / facilitateur@environnement.irisnet.be

SERVICES FOR INDIVIDUALS
The Urban Centre (Centre Urbain)
www.curbain.be
The Urban Centre provides free advice to any citizen of Brussels concerned for the sustainable urban development of his or her habitat. You will find there information and guidance on building renovation, energy saving and use of renewable energies, maintenance and preservation of the architectural heritage, the sound insulation of homes, and the eco-renovation of dwellings. An Urban Planning Facilitator (Faciliteur Urbanisme) is available for small projects.

PASSIVE PLATFORMS
www.maisonpassive.be / www.passiefhuisplatform.be
These platforms promote passive constructions towards all players in the construction process (individuals and professionals) and provide advice, information, research, certification and outreach. They provide certification of passive houses and organize training sessions throughout Belgium. They have also set up various services like assistance in calculating thermal bridges (www.ponts-thermiques.be) and an eco-balance sheet software (http://be-global.be).

BE.PASSIVE
be.passive is a quarterly magazine (in French) for professionals, devoted to passive and very low energy architecture. With stories on recent projects, interviews, technical articles, etc. All issues are available in PDF format on **www.bepassive.be**

[ACKNOWLEDGEMENTS]

This book is published under the leadership of Brussels Environment and the Brussels Ministry of the Environment, Energy and Urban Renewal.

It is published simultaneously in French under the title *A Bruxelles, les bâtiments exemplaires se racontent*, by the same publisher, and in Dutch under the title *Het verhaal achter de Voorbeeldgebouwen in Brussel* by Lannoo, Tielt.

Editorial board
Thanks to all the clients, architects, consulting engineers, building contractors and residents who participated in the "Batex" calls for projects, and in particular to those who were willing to share their experiences.

Thanks to Michelle Poskin and Astrid Legrand of Editions Racine, to Dominique Hambye, to Victor Levy and to Julie Willem, and also to the authors, Bernard Deprez and Jean Cech, for all the support work on the book.

Thanks to Yvan Glavie for the photography.

Particular thanks to Yasmina Baddi for the proofreading and to the entire "Bâtiments exemplaires" team of Brussels Environment.

JULIE TORRES MOSKOVITZ COPY

Photography
Unless otherwise stated, the computer graphics and plans are the property
of the authors of the projects.
All the photographs in the book are by Yvan Glavie, except:
Olivier Bruniels, p. 10-11
Bernard Deprez, p. 115, 209, 153 [141]
Georges de Kinder, p. 85
Filip Dujardin, p. 12, 40, 49, 55, 70, 75, 144, 157 photographies 2 and 3, 159, 173, 195
Victor Levy, p. 19, 25, 35, 59, 65, 77, 91, 99, 105, 123, 135, 143, 155, 167, 183, 197
MDW, p. 127 [004]
Synergy international, p. 188 [068]
Trait architectes, p. 137
Michel Wiegandt, p. 29 [005]
Julie Willem, p. 16 [071], 21 [091], 29 [112], 51, 67, 79, 93, 124, 127 [112], 150, 191

English Translation
Michael and Richard Lomax
Lay out
Dominique Hambye

www.racine.be
Register for our newsletter and receive information about our
publications and activities regularly.

© Editions Racine, 2012
Tour et Taxis, Entrepôt royal
86C, avenue du Port, BP 104A / B – 1000 Brussels

D. 2012, 6852. 37
Legal Registration: October 2012
ISBN 978-2-87386-800-0

This book was printed in Italy on FSC paper.